I WANT TO BE READY

I WANT TO BE READY

Improvised Dance as a Practice of Freedom

Danielle Goldman

THE UNIVERSITY OF MICHIGAN PRESS

ANN ARBOR

Copyright © 2010 by Danielle Goldman

Published in the United States of America by
The University of Michigan Press
Manufactured in the United States of America
⊗ Printed on acid-free paper

2013 2012 2011 2010   4 3 2 1

A CIP catalog record for this book is available from the British Library.

Library of Congress Cataloging-in-Publication Data

Goldman, Danielle.
   I want to be ready : improvised dance as a practice of freedom /
Danielle Goldman.
     p.   cm.
     Includes bibliographical references and index.
   ISBN 978-0-472-07084-8 (cloth : alk. paper) —
   ISBN 978-0-472-05084-0 (pbk. : alk. paper)
    1. Improvisation in dance.   2. Dance—Political aspects.
 I. Title.

  GV1781.2.G65   2010
  302.4'846—dc22   2009038401

  ISBN13 978-0-472-02661-6 (electronic)

To Ellis and Nick

Acknowledgments

I Want to Be Ready began as a dissertation in the Performance Studies Department at New York University. The project would not have been possible without the guidance of my dissertation committee: André Lepecki, Fred Moten, José Muñoz, and Tavia Nyong'o. I am grateful to them all for reading my work with such care. A special thanks goes to Barbara Browning, my advisor, for her support throughout this project, always delivered with eloquence and political clarity. I hope she will remain my advisor, always. Alex Vázquez aided this project in countless ways, helping me to clarify my thoughts while feeling sane along the way. Her work continues to inspire me. Christine Balance also offered many thoughtful comments. Randy Martin generously read the manuscript twice as it made its way from dissertation to book, and I am grateful for his encouragement and very helpful suggestions. My editor, Alison MacKeen, provided much insightful feedback and ushered the book through its various stages with great patience and skill.

Outside of NYU and the University of Michigan Press, many people have bolstered this project. Bob Green spent several late-night hours scanning and transcribing documents from Judith Dunn's "archive." Later, as I was revising this project, he welcomed me into his home in Vermont so I could look through the material in person. I am particularly grateful to Bill Dixon, who sent several photographs and later spent hours speaking with me about his eight-year collaboration with Judith Dunn. His work has a critical force that continues to be revelatory. Susan Sgorbati and Penny Campbell generously shared their experience working with Dunn and Dixon at Bennington, and Dianne McIntyre shared many wonderful stories of her work with musicians over the years. Taylor Ho Bynum read the manuscript from start to finish and offered many helpful comments, especially regarding my discussion of relations between music and dance.

My colleagues at The New School, in particular Stefania deKennessey, Jaime Santora, and Rebecca Stenn, as well as Jonathan Veitch, the dean of Eugene Lang College, have been a great source of support and have given me the opportunity to do work in which I truly believe. I have learned a great deal from my students at The New School, Barnard, and NYU, who have inspired and challenged me in complicated ways. My thinking owes a lot to Reginald Jackson and Noémie Solomon, who generously participated in my first graduate seminar and with whom I have had many wonderful conversations.

I also would like to thank the editorial board of *Women and Performance*—Barbara Browning, Joshua Chambers-Letson, Patricia Clough, Pamela Cobrin, Debra Levine, Ann Pellegrini, and Jeanne Vacarro—as well as Robert Diaz, Beth Kurkjian, Alex Pittman, and Paul Scolieri. The journal invited me to edit an issue dedicated to gendered relations between music and dance, which helped me to expand upon the issues raised in chapter 2. While I was revising this project, the journal's monthly meetings provided much-needed camaraderie and allowed me to feel as though my work is part of a shared project. Thank you to Ann Dils and *Dance Research Journal* for publishing portions of chapters 3 and 4. I also want to thank the 2004 Society of Dance History Scholars' Gertrude Lippincott Award Committee, whose encouragement helped me to think about relations between *Ghostcatching* and the politics of improvisation.

At a foundational level, this book would not exist without the many dance artists with whom I have worked in one way or another: Julie Alexander, Rachel Bernsen, Michelle Boulé, Frances Cohen, Mark Coniglio, Beth Gill, Levi Gonzalez, Miguel Gutierrez, Trajal Harrell, Deborah Hay, Lisa Herlinger-Thompson, Eleanor Houlihan, Juliette Mapp, Kayvon Pourazar, Judith Sánchez-Ruíz, Anna Sperber, Risa Steinberg, Dawn Stoppiello, Michou Szabo, and Sandy Tillett. A special thank you to DD Dorvillier and the cast of *Nottthing is Importanttt:* Martín Lanz Landazuri, Alejandra Martorell, Andrea Mauer, Paul Neuninger, Mina Nishimura, Otto Ramstad, Peter Sciscioli, and Elizabeth Ward.

Thanks to Laura Levine, who granted me the rights to reproduce an image of Dianne McIntyre, Max Roach, and Abbey Lincoln. Her photographs provide a rickety bridge back to an important performance of which very few traces remain. I also am grateful to Paul Kaiser for his *Ghostcatching* images and to Marta Braun for locating and scanning images of Etienne-Jules Marey on such short notice.

Finally, many thanks to my family. Special thanks to my parents, Margaret and Martin, and to Lisa, Michael, Susan, Zoe, Nina, Marshall, Phyllis, Heidi, and Scott. Their support keeps me grounded. I am endlessly grateful to Nick, who read the manuscript several times and endured much craziness, all while writing his own book. He is my most discerning, and loving, reader and friend. And of course there is Ellis, whose arrival has made the world a new place.

Contents

Introduction: The Land of the Free

In May of 2005, the choreographer David Dorfman was watching his Connecticut College seniors moving across the studio. "I just love the freedom of it, and if you don't like what you're doing, you can change it!" he exclaimed.[1] Dorfman's belief in the "freedom" of improvised dance is precisely what makes him so appealing to both students and faculty at the college. As the Dance Department's chairwoman explained, "We're all so fierce about our training. David brings in the improvisation and freedom aspect that is very welcome and desired."[2]

Such celebratory pairings of improvisation and freedom are common in the field of dance—not only in colleges but also among critics, scholars, and practicing artists across a range of genres. When attempting to define contact improvisation, Daniel Lepkoff, a central figure in the form's development, declared, "All the work leads to free duet dancing: together with a partner one freely explores movement possibilities."[3] Daniel Nagrin, the founder of the improvisational dance company The Workgroup and the author of *Dance and the Specific Image,* notes that his early training allowed for a "double facility": "I could improvise dance not only with freedom but with delight."[4] When discussing several well-known rhythm tap dancers, Jacqui Malone, an associate professor of drama, theater, and dance at Queens College and a former member of the Eleo Pomare Dance Company, wrote, "What these dancers value most is not the exactness of frozen choreography and set routines developed by others, but the joy that is inherent in improvisational flights of freedom."[5]

Although dance is the focus of this book, the tendency to link improvisation and freedom is not unique to the province of dance scholarship. In September 2007, the Center for Jazz Studies at Columbia University held an event to inaugurate its Conversation Series, a collection of public discussions initiated to explore the role of improvisation in a wide variety of fields. Fundamental to the Conversation Series is the belief that the study of improvisation can offer fresh models for scholarly inquiry and political action. The opening conversation, entitled "Improvisation in Everyday Life," featured a star-studded panel including the pianist Muhal Richard Abrams, the theater critic Margo Jefferson, the poet Yusef Komunyakaa, the composer and improviser George Lewis, and the law professor Patricia Williams. The panelists conflated jazz and improvisation throughout their conversation, treating the two as though they were equivalent, especially in their association with freedom. Komunyakaa's opening address described how jazz has affected his poetry: "The music signaled a kind of freedom, and that is what I internalized." Later he explained, "Jazz poetry demands trust in others, in the mode of freedom." And yet again he said, "I like the implied freedom that jazz brings to my work." Patricia Williams discussed jazz as a metaphor for inventive engagements with the law. Using jazz scores as a proxy for other kinds of life scripts, she remarked, "I associate jazz with a kind of freedom— a kind of breaking free."[6]

"Freedom" is a persistent fixture in discussions of improvisation and the arts—and yet its precise meaning is rarely examined. In fact, in most cases it seems to function as little more than shorthand, pointing toward something good with vaguely political implications. This casual use of language has real-world causes and effects, even in the seemingly self-contained realm of dance. As George Orwell argues in "Politics and the English Language," "[Language] becomes ugly and inaccurate because our thoughts are foolish, but the slovenliness of our language makes it easier for us to have foolish thoughts."[7] Orwell drew specific attention to sloppy invocations of "freedom," a term with a deep history in American politics—from the country's founding, through President Harry Truman's 1947 doctrine pledging America's support for "free peoples" everywhere, through President George Bush's twenty-two uses of the word at the 2004 Republican National Convention.[8] "Our nation's founding commitment is still our deepest commitment: In our world, and here at home, we will extend the frontiers of freedom," Bush said.[9] Although politicians almost always use the word ambiguously, they frequently imply that freedom is an ultimate destination or endpoint to which most of the world aspires.

I Want to Be Ready challenges this view, going against the grain of most written accounts of improvised dance to suggest that improvisation does not reflect or exemplify the understanding of freedom as a desired endpoint devoid of constraint. On the contrary, it actively resists it. Describing a middle section of *We Insist! The Freedom Now Suite* (1961), a performance that I discuss in chapter 2, the drummer Max Roach noted that he relished "the feeling of relaxed exhaustion after you've done everything you can to assert yourself. You can rest now because you've worked to be free."[10] Undoubtedly, the weight of history, institutional oppression, and Roach's desire for a more just world undergirds his claim. But the idea that one can achieve freedom once and for all, and that one can rest afterward, is problematic—not least because it elides the inevitably different ways in which different people imagine freedom. It seems likely, for example, that investment bankers, middle-class teenagers, factory workers, soccer moms, homeless people, and refugees harbor distinct pictures of freedom. Another problem with the idea of freedom-as-achievement is that it encourages and idealizes what is in effect a hardened stance to an inevitably changing world. It mistakenly suggests that if one could overcome a particular set of oppressions, all would be well, thereby eliding the fact that there are always multiple and diverse strictures in the world.

Deeply attuned to the force of shifting constraints, Fred Moten's recent work informs this book's discussion of improvised dance. In "Taste Flavor Dissonance Escape: Preface for a Solo by Miles Davis," Moten analyzes choreography in confinement though a discussion of Harriet Jacobs. Born into slavery, Jacobs hid from her sexually abusive owner by living for seven years in a crawlspace in her grandmother's attic before escaping to Philadelphia. Hers was perhaps the quintessential, and quite literal, *tight place* (a term I will use throughout the book to index various kinds of constraint): the garret in which she hid was a mere seven feet wide and nine feet long, with a sloping roof just three feet tall at its highest point. Although Jacobs could barely turn from one side to the other, her grandmother's crawlspace was also the space in which a series of ongoing and necessarily *improvisational* gestures took place—the secret acts of watching and listening to the outside world from which her written story eventually unfolded. Discussing *Incidents in the Life of a Slave Girl*, the famous narrative that Jacobs published in 1861 under the pseudonym Linda Brent, Moten explains: "[Jacobs's] is an amazing medley of shifts, a choreography in confinement . . . in a space [Nathanial] Mackey would characterize as cramped *and* capacious, a spacing

Jacques Derrida would recognize as a scene of writing, that Hortense Spillers has called a *scrawl* space."[11]

What is particularly interesting about Moten's discussion is the way in which it makes clear that Jacobs chose to live for seven years in a cramped attic, at grave risk to her health, rather than to accept life as a slave. Jacobs also mentions, toward the end of her narrative, that having her freedom bought for her tarnished the triumph of escape: "I felt grateful for the kindness that prompted this offer, but the idea was not so pleasant to me as might have been expected. The more my mind had become enlightened, the more difficult it was for me to consider myself an article of property; and to pay money to those who had so grievously oppressed me seemed like taking from sufferings the glory of triumph."[12] Escape for Jacobs always meant flight from a regime of exchange. According to Moten, if Jacobs's freedom could only come by way of exchange, she would need to escape from freedom too.[13]

The suggestion that one could escape confinement only to enter into or become aware of another set of strictures (a state of affairs that exists well beyond the historical institution of slavery) is vital to understanding the political power of improvisation. As Michel Foucault suggests in his late writings and interviews, one must be careful when speaking of liberation. Foucault understood that liberation is often urgent and necessary. But he also insisted that it is never sufficient for creating full forms of existence. Instead he emphasized the need for "practices of freedom":

> I am not trying to say that liberation as such, or this or that form of liberation, does not exist: when a colonized people attempts to liberate itself from its colonizers, this is indeed a practice of liberation in the strict sense. But we know very well, and moreover in this specific case, that this practice of liberation is not in itself sufficient to define the practices of freedom that will still be needed if this people, this society, and these individuals are to be able to define admissible and acceptable forms of existence or political society. This is why I emphasize practices of freedom over processes of liberation.[14]

Throughout *I Want to Be Ready,* but most explicitly in the final chapter, I posit improvised dance as a Foucauldian practice that resists the hardened stance (whether described as complacency, deserved relaxation, or celebration) that comes with the reification of freedom. To that end, the book presents a series of case studies that emphasize the shifting constraints that improvisers negotiate, arguing that one's social and historical positions in the world affect one's ability to move, both literally and figuratively. The case studies include mambo dancing at New York's Palladium Ballroom, collaborations between dancers and jazz musicians, relations between contact improvisation and techniques of nonviolent protest, and the role of improvisation in the performances of Bill T. Jones. Together they illustrate that to ignore the constraints that improvisers inevitably encounter is not only to deny the real conditions that shape daily life; it is also to deny improvisation's most significant power as a full-bodied critical engagement with the world, characterized by both flexibility and perpetual readiness.

After countless hours watching both live and recorded improvisations (and having been moved greatly in the process), I have come to believe that improvised dance involves literally giving shape to oneself by deciding how to move in relation to an unsteady landscape. To engage oneself in this manner, with a sense of confidence and possibility, is a powerful way to inhabit one's body and to interact with the world.

"Who Moves? Who Doesn't?"

Improvisation is generally described as a spontaneous mode of creation that takes place without the aid of a manuscript or score. According to this view, performance and composition occur simultaneously—on the spot—through a practice that values surprise, innovation, and the vicissitudes of process rather than the fixed glory of a finished product. This view may initially seem straightforward, but, as I hope this book makes clear, it becomes increasingly complicated the more instances of improvisation one considers. As the ethnomusicologist Paul Berliner states in *Thinking in Jazz,* composition and improvisation "overlap hopelessly at the margins."[15] Many improvisers work with loose scores, call upon idiomatic tradition, or cultivate individual styles. And many compositions begin with improvisation.

A more serious problem with many discussions of improvisation is that their emphasis on spontaneity and intuition often implies a lack of preparation, thereby eliding the historical knowledge, the sense of tradition, and the enormous skill that the most eloquent improvisers are able to mobilize. As the musician Arthur Rhames explains, "Improvisation is an intuitive process for me now, but . . . I'm calling upon all the resources of all the years of my playing at once: my academic understanding of the music, my historical understanding of the music, and my technical understanding of the instrument that I'm playing."[16] Influenced by improvisers such as Rhames, this study highlights the ways in which dancers learn to improvise and hone their skills. In so doing, it also underscores the need to distinguish the speed and spontaneity of skilled improvisation from a simple lack of preparation.

Most important, as discussed earlier, this project analyzes the shifting social, historical, and material conditions in which dancing occurs. I refer to these constraints throughout *I Want to Be Ready* as "tight places," a phrase that comes from Houston Baker's book *Turning South Again*. In *Turning South Again*, Baker relates incarceration to African Americans' struggle to participate fully in modernism, a struggle that Baker argues is defined by citizenship and, also, mobility. From slave ships to the current prison system, incarceration has, according to Baker, significantly shaped black experience in the United States. But the phrase "tight places" nevertheless suggests something far subtler than literal lock-ups. One of Baker's most dynamic examples comes from Booker T. Washington, who was asked to speak in Georgia in front of an audience of both whites and blacks from the North and South in 1895. Feeling as though he was heading toward the gallows on the morning he was to present his speech, Washington was approached by a white farmer. The farmer pronounced, "Washington, you have spoken before the Northern white people, the Negroes in the South; but in Atlanta, tomorrow, you will have before you the Northern whites, the Southern whites, and the Negroes all together. I am afraid that you have got into a tight place."[17]

In adopting Baker's term, I do not by any means wish to equate all types of constraint. Some spaces are obviously "tighter" than others, and I am interested in a range of constraints that involve race but also class, gender, sexuality, time, and even artistic conventions. Nevertheless, Baker's term offers a useful starting place from which to analyze the ways in which one's shifting social and historical positions in the world affect one's mobility. Inevitably, people move differently in different contexts, and having to negotiate these various contexts at once can be extremely difficult or fraught. As illustrated by Baker's discussion of Booker T. Washington, the inevitable compromises or concessions that people make in one particular context become increasingly difficult when they occupy diverse settings, or must perform before diverse constituencies, at once. Baker defines tight places in various ways and gives multiple examples throughout his book, but he summarizes his definition by describing tight places as "the always ambivalent cultural compromises of occupancy and vacancy, differentially affected by contexts of situations."[18] He then poses a crucial question with tremendous importance for dance scholarship: that is, "Who moves? Who doesn't?"[19]

Despite the weight of these questions, they are frequently absent in studies of social dance. To a certain extent, Cynthia Novack's *Sharing the Dance: Contact Improvisation and American Culture* recognizes the significance of context in its discussion of rock-and-roll dancing. Novack notes that although many people experienced their dancing as "free" during the 1960s, structural and stylistic norms still influenced their movement. She also states, "Depending on the circumstances and cultural backgrounds of the participants or observers, different aspects of the dancing would emerge as primary."[20] Still, Novack's discussion of social dance fails to pay adequate attention to the racial divisions that characterized the United States during the early 1960s. Far more than her title or brief discussion allows, the story of social dancing in the United States at midcentury involved complicated instances of appropriation and exclusion. It certainly was *not* a simple tale of integration and sharing. And when Novack states that "the movement qualities of rock dancing were also associated with contemporary social movements and practices such as the civil rights movement, youth culture, and drug-taking, and with values such as rebellion, expressiveness, and individualism within a loving community of peers," one wonders how far this "loving community of peers" extended.[21]

In *Steppin' on the Blues: The Visible Rhythms of African American Dance*, Jacqui Malone recognizes that vernacular dance, especially in African American traditions, requires both spontaneity and control.[22] But in her discussion of slave dancing, which spawned many later forms of social dance, she describes slaves as enjoying an "improvisational flair" that separated their dancing from the plantation owners' stagnant notions about dance.[23] The impression that improvised dance under slavery was a matter of aesthetic flourish is complicated by Saidiya Hartman's analysis of forced entertainment under the institution of slavery. In *Scenes of Subjection: Terror, Slavery, and Self-Making in Nineteenth-Century America*, Hartman demonstrates the convergence of terror and enjoyment that occurred in many scenes of slave dancing and emphasizes that any "improvisational flair" that may have existed was entwined with systems of discipline and domination.

Anthony Shay's *Choreophobia: Solo Improvised Dance in the Iranian*

World makes an important intervention in the field of dance studies not only by showing the risks and uncertainty of improvised dance but also by highlighting the importance of context when analyzing the political significance of any physical practice. Although the Islamic Republic banned all dancing after the 1979 revolution, solo improvisations remain widespread in private and, according to Shay, create an important "space for resistance to the regime."[24] Perhaps most relevant to this study, though, is the way Shay demonstrates that the same dancing can mean different things for different people in different contexts. In other words, deciding whether an individual's solo improvised dance is normative, transgressive, or what he calls "out-of-control" requires a look at several factors: individual personality, context, gender, age, social class, and religiosity.[25] In one of his vivid examples, Shay explains that in contemporary Iran it means something different for an older, well-respected woman to dance in a "sexy" manner at a party than for a scantily clad young woman to do so. Shay describes an instance where an elderly woman generally thought to be "prim" shocked partygoers by swiveling her head, moving her hips, and throwing imaginary breasts in the air. By dancing in this way, she exhibited a "sexiness" that was at odds with her normal mode of public behavior and, according to Shay, mildly transgressive. At the same party, a woman in her forties also danced with abandon in a way that differed from her typical demeanor. She made direct eye contact with men, moved her pelvis vigorously, and wore a thin summer dress with little underneath. According to Shay, whereas people found the older woman's behavior to be unusual but amusing, they were shocked by the younger woman's performance and described her as "out of control" and possibly on drugs.[26]

Along with the social-historical and material conditions that affect how people move, physical technique constitutes another "tight place" that is crucial to my analysis. Technique enables eloquent articulation in dance. But it also shapes the body's contours and enforces ways of moving. Steve Paxton, one of dance improvisation's greatest champions, usefully describes how habits and learned techniques make it difficult to move in surprising or unfamiliar ways: "I spent many years studying dance and in that time, I became brainwashed. . . . I came out of the Cunningham Company and I couldn't stop pointing my toe. That's the problem. We are creatures of physical habit."[27] In *Critical Moves: Dance Studies in Theory and Politics,* Randy Martin builds upon this observation by noting that all bodies house a multiplicity of techniques, which dancers mediate based on the demands of a given situation or choreographer.[28] According to Martin, these techniques frequently interfere with each other. Elegant dancers in one idiom often struggle as they move to an unfamiliar form. For example, it is generally hard for a classically trained ballet dancer to collapse quickly to the ground (since ballet training emphasizes verticality and lift); likewise it is often difficult for a modern dancer to extend his or her leg in an exalted arabesque (since training often focuses on groundedness). Although dancers occasionally become frustrated when techniques interfere with one another, they are not always aware of a technique's hold, even when traces remain evident for outside observers.[29] This tension is precisely what drives the popular FOX TV show *So You Think You Can Dance,* where performers trained in forms ranging from clogging to crumping to ballet to ballroom alternate between idioms in the hopes that the public will deem them "America's Favorite Dancer."

By no means peculiar to professional dancers, physical techniques also are learned outside the studio, and this has implications that extend well beyond concert stages.[30] All too often, discussions of improvisation and freedom in dance literature assume that freedom from dance conventions entails freedom from social conventions or political norms in general, when in fact the relations between these spheres are dynamic and complex. As each chapter of this study attempts to make clear, one does not check one's "everyday body" at the door upon entering a studio or concert hall, and one's artistic choices are never entirely separate from the broader social world in which one lives. Consider, for example, the fact that many of the white dancers associated with the Judson Dance Theater in New York during the early 1960s considered pedestrian activities such as walking and standing to be respectable art and appropriate for downtown stages; meanwhile, many of the black dancers in New York found some sense of liberation in the formal techniques and virtuosity of modern dance, which opened up previously inaccessible high-art stages.

In 1934, the French sociologist Marcel Mauss wrote an essay entitled "Techniques of the Body," which analyzes how movement tendencies develop in daily life. Attempting to organize a set of observations about human movement that ethnographic studies had thus far reduced to mere "miscellanea," Mauss begins with the case of swimming: "I was well aware that walking or swimming, for example, and all sorts of things of the same type are specific to determinate societies; that the Polynesians do not swim as we do, that my generation did not swim as the present generation does."[31]

Moreover, he exclaims that despite realizing the stupidity of the outdated technique of swallowing water and spitting it back out, he still did it. "I cannot get rid of my technique," he says.[32] Throughout the essay, Mauss describes various ways of moving—walking, eating, running, climbing, resting, and even giving birth—arguing that people have habitual ways of moving that "vary especially between societies, educations, proprieties and fashions, and types of prestige."[33]

In the course of his discussion, Mauss challenges the notion that there are natural ways of moving, reminding readers that behavior is rewarded or punished in both subtle and extreme ways. He recalls an early teacher shouting at him: "Idiot! Why do you walk around the whole time with your hands flapping wide open?" Such pronouncements—dictating what is polite or appropriate, what is graceful, what is efficient—constitute our bodily education, and that education is extremely context-dependent. For example, as Mauss points out, the act of staring fixedly would be "a symbol of politeness in the army, and of rudeness in everyday life."[34] The norms dictating appropriate bodily movement often relate to aspects of one's identity, including race, gender, age, and sexuality. But a skilled improviser will be intimately familiar with her habitual ways of moving, as well as with the shifting social norms that give those movements meaning. Then, on a moment-to-moment basis, she figures out how to move.

An Art That Is "Hard to Catch"

In *At the Vanishing Point, A Critic Looks at Dance,* Marcia Siegel voices the widely held belief that dance constitutes the ephemeral art par excellence. "No other art is so hard to catch," she writes, "so impossible to hold."[35] This belief has played an important role in the historically low status of dance as an institution. As André Lepecki writes, "The whole project of dance theory can be summarized as follows: dance vanishes; it does not 'stay around' (for such is the unfortunate condition of its materiality); therefore, the dance scholar, theorist, critic, must work against dance's materiality by fixating the dance."[36] Given that not even Labanotation, one of the most sophisticated systems for analyzing and recording human movement, is part of a regular pedagogy or general cultural knowledge, the pervasive sentiment that systems of notation can never adequately capture the complexity of improvised performance is particularly acute for dance. So, if dance is low on the totem pole, improvised dance is even lower.

Nonetheless, some scholars have taken a different approach. In the final chapter of *Exhausting Dance,* Lepecki argues that the project of striving to fixate dance has been decidedly melancholic and paralyzing for dance scholarship. He then suggests that nonpsychoanalytic models of temporality (such as those offered by Henri Bergson and Gilles Deleuze) might offer a useful alternative for dance studies. Following Bergson, Lepecki asks: what if the past was not an ever-growing trove of passing instants, but rather *"that which acts no longer?"*[37] This view opens one up to the continuing effects of dance, even after its visual disappearance or what some might consider its end.

Lepecki is not alone in his attempt to embrace the ephemerality of dance. Mark Franko contends that one must not deny dance's ephemerality; instead one should recuperate it as a powerful trope, a critical gesture that Franko attributes to deconstruction and, especially, Jacques Derrida's understanding of "trace."[38] Particularly relevant to the concerns of this book, Lepecki argues that the Derridean embrace of ephemerality constitutes an embrace of *improvisation* as well. Lepecki explains: "For Derrida, only when dance happens off the record, beyond registration, when it escapes from the trap of documentation, when it vanishes into time properly, when it steps outside history—only then does it generate a powerful disturbance within the field of signification. That is to say: for Derrida, dance must be improvised, must move before writing."[39]

Although the claim that improvised dance holds the potential to cause radical disturbance is compelling, it remains to be seen why, as Lepecki writes, improvisation must "escape the trap of documentation."[40] For here, too, improvisation is tacitly defined in opposition to documentation and recorded history.[41] So what then is at stake in this claim? Is it possible for dancers to "step outside history," and to what end? As José Muñoz writes, "To be only in 'the live' means that one is denied history and futurity."[42] Recognizing that it is not always in one's best interest to leave too many traces, he also argues that it is both a privilege and a pleasure to be a part of recorded history. I discuss these issues at length in chapter 2, when analyzing the political significance of improvised collaborations between the choreographer Judith Dunn and the trumpeter Bill Dixon, and between the choreographer Dianne McIntyre and various musicians including Cecil Taylor, Max Roach, and Abbey Lincoln. The improvisational practices that these artists developed challenged typical divisions between "high" and "low" forms of expression, gendered relations between postmodern dance and jazz, and the assumed whiteness of the avant-garde. Yet very few traces of these ventures remain. When I asked Dixon why his work with Judith Dunn is largely absent from history books, he quipped, "The history that gets written is the history that's permissible."[43]

Rather than romanticizing some realm "outside of history," this project demonstrates that the value of being a historical subject is not something that one easily can dismiss. It also underscores the need to consider context when analyzing the politics of any physical practice. To echo Houston Baker's fundamental question yet again, *who moves, and who doesn't?* What expectations are placed on which kinds of bodies, and why? Throughout this study, I emphasize the materiality of dancing bodies and try to ground each example of improvisation in a variety of specific and complicated contexts. I also acknowledge the political significance of documentation and the frequent necessity and evidentiary potential of ephemera.[44] This study would be impossible without the aid of recording devices: each chapter depends upon photographs, sound recordings, and videos—all that remains after improvisation has taken place.

More than Whimsy: Cross-Cultural Contact and Collaboration

Although *I Want to Be Ready* focuses on a series of historically specific moments, it is not a traditional work of cultural history. Instead of presenting a linear and continuous narrative, the chapters juxtapose important explorations in improvised dance. Taken together, these explorations enable a sustained analysis of varied social, cultural, and historical constraints that will, I hope, make clear that the questions improvisation raises are central to both dance studies and to any attempt to relate dance to politics.

People frequently use the terms *modern* and *postmodern* when speaking about the arts, but the terms take on specific meanings and become notably more complicated when applied to dance. In *Terpsichore in Sneakers*, Sally Banes notes that when dancers such as Yvonne Rainer, Trisha Brown, and Steve Paxton started using the term *postmodern* to describe their work at Judson Church in New York and other places in the early 1960s, they were primarily concerned with indicating a chronological rupture. Their generation followed, and wanted to break with, the group of individuals known as modern dancers. But, according to Banes, "historical modern dance was never really *modernist*."[45] The modernist interest in abstraction and materiality actually emerged among the self-proclaimed postmodern dancers, many of whom were inspired by, and viewed their work in relation to, minimalist sculpture.[46] Thus, according to Banes, the fact that dance was antimodern did not necessarily mean that it was antimodernist. Yet postmodern dancers did hold many postmodernist interests: the use of vernacular forms and an interest in other cultures, in challenging the boundaries between art and everyday life, and in process rather than product.[47] They also turned to improvisation as a provocative mode of dance making.

Despite these complexities, both scholars and dancers speak of modern and postmodern dance to loosely indicate distinct historical moments and as shorthand for particular individuals. John Martin, the *New York Times* dance critic from 1927 until 1962, played a major role in establishing this usage. In 1931–32, Martin gave a series of lectures at the New School for Social Research, which was later published as *The Modern Dance*. In his lectures, books, and writings for the *Times,* Martin gave a name to a theatrical brand of dance that was developing in Broadway and off-Broadway theaters, usually on Sunday afternoons when theaters were vacant.[48] At the time, people were apparently unsure what to make of this dancing. According to Martin, "The dance has only recently begun to be recognized as a major art and there is still considerable confusion about it, not only in the public mind, but in the minds of the dancers themselves as a class."[49] He therefore tried to explain and advocate for the work being done by dancers such as Martha Graham, Doris Humphrey, Helen Tamiris, and Mary Wigman as well as the earlier work of Isadora Duncan and Ruth St. Denis (even though they didn't refer to their dance as "modern").[50]

Martin's writings echoed the dancing he discussed by attempting to elevate the status of dance as an art form. Whether because of its ephemerality, its embodied character, its association with femininity, or a combination of all these things, U.S. cultural critics seldom took dance seriously. When considering the relation between dance and the other "major" arts (music, drama, poetry, painting, sculpture, and architecture), Martin explained that people tended to rank dance with "subsidiary" arts such as landscape gardening and basket weaving. Martin attributed this to the fact that dance was subsumed by and existed primarily within the boundaries of music. In an effort to correct this tendency to subsume dance to music, he tried to isolate the essence of dance, which he identified as movement. Interestingly, in so doing, Martin engaged in precisely the kind of modernist project that Banes claims was absent in dance from the 1930s and 1940s.[51] Martin writes:

> [The modern dance] has set itself positively against the artifice of the classic ballet, making its chief aim the expression of an inner compulsion; but it has also seen the necessity for vital forms for this expression, and indeed has realized the aesthetic value of form in and of itself as an adjunct to this expression. In carrying out this purpose it has thrown aside everything that has gone before and started all over again from the beginning. The beginning was the discovery of the actual substance of the dance, which it found to be movement.[52]

In Martin's discussion, one sees a conflation of dance and movement, as well as the modernist trope of new beginnings, both of which have been challenged in recent studies.[53] As Randy Martin argues in *Critical Moves,* "modern dance develops as a very complex matrix of appropriations of different movement sources, not the least of which are dance expressions generated by those subject to [U.S.] colonization and enslavement."[54] The challenge now is to take our cues from scholars such as Randy Martin by thinking rigorously about appropriation while also analyzing productive, but often ignored, instances of cross-cultural contact and collaboration.

To a certain extent, this work has begun. Susan Manning, for example, urges scholars to acknowledge the many intercultural fusions that have shaped U.S. concert dance—not merely those that fall into a reductive black/white binary—and to ask why these performances and moments of contact have been elided in official histories.[55] Ann Dils and Ann Cooper Albright engage in a similar project in *Moving History/Dancing Cultures: A Dance History Reader.* Rather than presenting modern dance as merely an American rejection of European ballet, Dils and Albright urge their readers to consider connections between modern dance and other forms of movement and to be international in scope. Perhaps most important, addressing an issue that is particularly salient in this book's discussion of mambo, Dils and Albright emphasize the ethical problems and faulty logic involved in framing some dance forms as historical and others as anthropological.[56] Reflecting on their own training as dance scholars, they explain: "Presenting some dance forms as history and others as anthropology created a sense that some dances were art, and perhaps of higher complexity or status, and some dances simply expressions of social behavior or religious belief."[57]

Brenda Dixon Gottschild's *The Black Dancing Body,* published in 2003, furthers this project. Exploring conceptions of "black dance" and the "black dancing body," Gottschild argues that the only way out of habitual cultural biases and racial stereotypes is to go through them—to air them out and analyze them. Early in her book, Gottschild exclaims: "Here we are, living in the twenty-first century, talking about black dance and black dancers! What are we really talking about?"[58] Through interviews with twenty-four contemporary dancers of various races and ethnicities, performance analysis, and reflections on her own experience as a black female dancer, Gottschild charts the "geography" of the black dancing body. She analyzes racial stereotypes surrounding feet, hair, lips, butt, and skin. In the end, she argues that, although there is no such thing as inherently "black dance" or "white dance," the "habit of racism has rendered us unable to put the fusion of American cultural creations into words from the vocabulary at our disposal."[59]

I hope my work will contribute to the further "airing out" of cultural biases by highlighting some of the formal intersections and instances of cross-cultural contact overlooked in published dance history. Paying particular attention to questions of identity as well as the politics of form, this book analyzes significant instances in which dancers worked across difference, bringing to the fore issues of appropriation, cultural belonging, misunderstanding, and, at times, stunning collaborations. Such critical scholarship shifts standard narratives of improvisation's significance in necessary ways. For one, it reveals that while many people have experienced improvisation as politically significant, it does not offer identical modes or degrees of resistance for everyone involved.[60] At the same time, simplistic origin myths begin to collapse in ways that make clear that the postmodernist interest in improvisation did not begin with the Judson Dance Theater, as is frequently implied.

Although this study in no way purports to be historically comprehensive, there is nevertheless a chronological dimension that warrants discussion. Each chapter explores dancing from the latter half of the twentieth century precisely because improvisation seldom appeared on stage before that time in the United States. Admittedly, early twentieth-century modern dancers improvised in the early stages of making a dance, or in order to investigate movement ideas and develop technical principals. But they seldom improvised *on stage*. Struggling to "elevate" dance from the realms of vaudeville or exercise or social dance to a so-called serious art, dancers often dismissed improvisation as a form of "amateur self-expression."[61] This dismissive attitude was a product of gender and racial biases. Susan Foster explains that while improvisation has been linked with femininity across artistic disciplines, this link is especially acute in improvised dance, which is more obviously an art of the body than other forms. Foster writes:

> Music's visible abundance of "structure," its close alliance with mathematics, and the viability of its notation system carried a masculine valence that contrasted with dance's feminine ephemerality and bodiliness. Theater likewise boasted the enduring and structurally complex text as the foundation of any performance, whereas dance's choreography defied the printed page. Enjoying the full range of stereotypic attributes associated with the feminine, dance was often viewed as ornamental or sensual, chaotic or emotional, fecund but insubstantial. To improvise within music or theater thus signaled a departure from structural integrity, but not a complete abandonment of structural principles. In dance, however, the act of improvising often connoted an even deeper immersion in the chaotic evanescence of physicality, one that was dismissed as insignificant by many.[62]

Moreover, many improvisatory traditions have deep roots in non-Western traditions of dance and music. This history makes it hard to ignore the racism embedded in the claim that improvisation somehow lacks rigor or in the equation of improvisational skill with instinct as opposed to intellect, both prevalent notions in the early-to-mid-twentieth century. Even as postmodern dancers during the early 1960s began to incorporate improvisation into their performances, often noting the influence of Zen philosophy or Asian martial arts, they frequently failed to acknowledge the importance of jazz and black social dance traditions in their so-called innovations. Although it is unclear whether this cultural disavowal was self-consciously strategic, it was undoubtedly racially significant.

A similar elision occurs in a great deal of dance scholarship, especially those studies that recognize the complicated relationships that existed between improvised dance and the freedom struggles that were taking place in the United States during the latter half of the twentieth century. This is where Sally Banes's *Greenwich Village 1963: Avant-Garde Performance and the Effervescent Body* is both suggestive and problematic. It attempts to place the appeal of improvisation within a specific historical moment and location and gives a culturally one-sided sense that the experience of "freedom" felt by a group of white avant-garde artists extended to America as a whole. Attempting to portray the spirit of 1963, Banes describes an overly buoyant hopefulness. She states: "In 1963 the American Dream of freedom, equality, and abundance seemed as if it could come true. Not that it had—but that it was just about to. . . . There was a feeling—so unlike the early 1990s—that all things were possible . . . and permitted."[63] It is difficult, however, to imagine a universal sense that in 1963 all things were possible and permitted. Yes, as Banes notes, 1963 was the year of the famous March on Washington. But it was also the year when Martin Luther King Jr. was jailed in Birmingham and when four young black girls were killed by a bombing at Birmingham's Sixteenth Street Baptist Church, the location of many civil rights meetings. When Banes acknowledges the civil rights struggle, she exclaims, "Genuine freedom seemed around the corner for African Americans."[64] Perhaps, but the struggle was messy, and difficult, and a long time coming. She claims that the civil rights movement "operated in an arena of hope" and that "it is in the context of that hopeful passion and sense of imminent liberation that blacks and with them, white liberals, intellectuals, and artists felt an entire culture buoyed in ways both direct and indirect."[65] According to Banes, "Officially, it was a time of consensus. And the consensus was that life in the United States was good—and getting better."[66]

As this suggests, Banes uses black freedom struggles to establish an "American sensibility" that she claims pulsed through the avant-garde art world of 1963. But the artists discussed by Banes are overwhelmingly white, and there does not seem to be any attention paid to the black artists who so clearly viewed their art as propelled by a freedom drive. She mentions the Judson Dance Theater, Pop Art, the Living Theater, the pop movies of Andy Warhol, Kenneth Anger, and Jack Smith, Fluxus, and Charlotte Moorman. But for all her talk of an avant-garde movement buoyed by a hope for freedom, epitomized in the civil rights movement, there is scant mention of jazz or any of the black artists making radical work in the 1960s. When Banes does engage with this work, she focuses primarily on theater, and she relegates the discussion to "Black Art and Art about Blacks," a thirteen-page section of a chapter entitled *Dreaming Freedoms*.

In this respect, Scott Saul's *Freedom Is, Freedom Ain't: Jazz and the Making of the Sixties* offers an important counterpoint to Banes. Saul's book analyzes the craft and aesthetic choices made by jazz musicians between the mid-1950s and the mid-1960s. Looking to music like Miles Davis's *Birth of the Cool,* Max Roach's *Freedom Now Suite,* Charles Mingus's *The Black Saint and the Sinner Lady,* and John Coltrane's *A Love Supreme,* Saul argues that these artists made formal choices regarding musical arrangement, genre,

and improvisation that opened new musical vistas and enabled artists to en-
act "new stances to the world."[67] Saul describes the music in detail, determined throughout to link aesthetic choices to the social world that gave the
music its "meaning, charge, and relevance."[68] The picture offered by Saul differs significantly from the "buoyant hopefulness" that Banes argues characterized 1963. Nowhere in Saul's text does one see a "time of consensus"
where an "official mood" prevailed. Rather, he discusses the many ways in
which the term *freedom* was employed during the 1950s and 1960s, from
Cold War security documents such as NSC 68, to treatises by democratic the-
orists such as Isaiah Berlin, to celebrations of economic free enterprise, to
artistic choices within the avant-garde, to the civil rights movement. According to Saul, *freedom* operated in this period as a beloved but also hotly con-
tested term.

Perhaps the starkest contrast between Saul and Banes emerges in Saul's
introduction, as he analyzes Mingus's scored poem "Freedom," first performed in 1962 to the alternating rhythm of a chain gang. According to Saul,
"jazz artists wanted to claim the banner of freedom, but they also wanted to
distance themselves from the term's association with individual license and
whimsical choice. The pursuit of freedom, in Mingus's poem, is hard work if
nothing else."[69] Saul notes that the poem, which ends with the line "But no
freedom for me," simultaneously "celebrates and chokes" on the promise of
freedom.[70] In addition to the emphasis on work, the virtues of struggle, and
a coexistent sense of celebration and choking, Saul notes that the conception
of freedom present in hard bop and the civil rights movement was deeply social and rooted in collaborative action. According to Saul, "The dynamism of
hard bop depended on the tension and interplay between the members of the
group; jazz musicians presumed that their band mates would press upon their
own sense of freedom. When one musician 'infringed' on the rhythm or har-
monic space of another musician, it was usefully reconceived as a provoca-
tion, a license for bold counter-response."[71]

The literature on jazz complicates understandings of improvised dance in
the United States because, in general, it presents a more exacting look at race
and the politics of performance during the 1960s and 1970s than typically appears in dance studies. Moreover, it is in the literature on jazz, and of course
in the music itself, that one can find a vast and rigorous analysis of improvisation. Derek Bailey's *Improvisation: Its Nature and Practice in Music;* Paul
Berliner's *Thinking in Jazz: The Infinite Art of Improvisation;* LeRoi Jones's

Blues People and *Black Music; The Jazz Cadence of American Culture,*
edited by Robert O'Meally; Scott Saul's *Freedom Is, Freedom Ain't: Jazz and
the Making of the Sixties;* and writings by Bill Dixon have aided this study.
One problem, however, is that jazz literature tends to discuss race and blackness primarily in relation to the straight African American male, creating a
narrow, binary view of race that overlooks aspects of identity such as gender
and sexuality, as well as the complexity of diasporic cultural production.
Fred Moten's *In the Break: The Aesthetics of the Black Radical Tradition;*
Farah Jasmine Griffin's *If You Can't Be Free, Be a Mystery: In Search of Billie Holiday;* Gayle Jones's *Corregidora;* Angela Davis's *Blues Legacies and
Black Feminism: Gertrude "Ma" Rainey, Bessie Smith, and Billie Holiday;*
Nathaniel Mackey's "Cante Moro"; and Lisa Brock and Digna Castañeda
Fuertes's *Between Race and Empire: African-Americans and Cubans before
the Cuban Revolution* suggest in different ways the limits of such a reduction
and are vitally important in this book.

Directing One's Choreographic Critique

In *African-American Concert Dance,* John Perpener discusses the reasons why
so many black choreographers in the United States adhered to modern dance
aesthetics and modes of production during the 1960s and 1970s instead of embracing the projects of the Judson Dance Theater or contact improvisation:

> Among these reasons is the likelihood that black artists were not en-
> thralled with the idea of rejecting the traditions they had struggled so
> hard to become a part of just a few years earlier. They—unlike the coterie
> of white artists who were committed to aesthetic change—found little
> transgressive pleasure in dismantling the established practices of modern
> dance. . . . African-American artists could hardly relate to the notion that
> they needed to repudiate the hegemony of historical modern dance aes-
> thetics because it restricted their creative freedom. Moreover, they were
> reminded, at every turn, of the tenuous nature of their involvement in the
> mainstream dance world that avant-garde white artists were rejecting.[72]

Perpener suggests that if one is to consider dancers' choreographic choices,
one also ought to consider the dancers' institutional position and broader social standing. In other words, which aesthetic choices and artistic means are
available to whom and at what cost? What issues are most pressing when deciding how to move? Where is one's choreographic critique directed?

Throughout *I Want to Be Ready*, improvisers negotiate their relation to institutions of dance and social networks in a landscape akin to what Pierre Bourdieu has called an "artistic field." Bourdieu describes literature as "a veritable social universe . . . of entirely specific struggles, notably concerning the question of knowing who is part of the universe, who is a real writer and who is not."[73] Likening the constraints of an artistic field to a kind of imprisonment, Bourdieu suggests that artists' creative projects, by no means mechanistically determined, depend upon an awareness of these strictures and one's shifting, but historically produced, social standing.[74] I have tried to expose the exclusionary nature of such a field while also examining its fissures and fault lines. While examples abound, perhaps the most explicit point of tension exists in chapter 3, in a heated conversation between Steve Paxton and Bill T. Jones that took place after the two artists performed solos for a Movement Research Studies Project in 1983.[75] At times angry, insecure, and insulted, the two brilliant artists hashed out their relations to a particular tradition of modern and postmodern U.S. concert dance. Jones, feeling alienated from the contact improvisation scene that Paxton helped to found, suggested that because of pervasive prejudice some dancers were on the inside of the clique, while others were not. A bit later in the conversation, Paxton, an avid and well-known improviser, failed to recognize that the spoken text in Jones's solo had been improvised, a misrecognition that raises significant questions about improvisation's role in postmodern dance: What does improvised dance look like? And whose tradition is it? Of course, the suggestion that improvisation *looks* a certain way obscures its power as a mode rather than a product, hardened and made legible by distinctive aesthetic characteristics.

In addition to complicating those histories that unthinkingly isolate "black dance" as something separate from the aesthetic avant-garde, *I Want to Be Ready* also complicates simple divisions between dance and everyday life. In each chapter, the notion that pure form exists in dance, or the idea mentioned in the previous discussion of technique that one might step onto the stage and leave one's daily body behind, begins to crumble. Many of the artists discussed in the book (Judith Dunn, Bill Dixon, Katherine Dunham, Dianne McIntyre, Bill T. Jones, Steve Paxton, and Esmeralda Santiago, among others) were affected and to varying degrees radicalized by the social and political events of their day, including the women's liberation movement, the civil rights movement, immigration policy, poverty, and the Vietnam War.

In many cases, dancers' improvisational responses to worldly events were mediated by, and expressed to a great extent through, dance conventions. The performers used improvisation as a way to criticize the ways in which institutions supported certain kinds of dance, as well as notions about the autonomy of dance as an art form. In particular, their improvisations challenged the ways in which formalism in dance historically has effaced struggle (by privileging grace and verticality and by excluding the outside world). Scholars such as Bourdieu have noted that dominant aesthetic tastes often measure and evaluate works of art by their distance from necessity. But many of the artists discussed in this book improvised in an attempt to bring necessity into the picture, using it to challenge the conservatism of the dance world itself.[76]

Whether this avant-gardism limited the general legibility of their danced interactions with the world remains a vexed question, and many of the dancers were explicitly aware of this tension. For example, in the discussion mentioned earlier between Bill T. Jones and Steve Paxton, Jones explained that he found many postmodern dance experiments to be "ungenerous."[77] Rather than performing subtle improvised explorations for a handful of like-minded and similarly trained people, Jones wanted to perform in big theaters, for large audiences, making dances that lots of people would understand. But during the late 1990s, Jones began to grapple with an emerging desire for "pure" form or aesthetics, on the one hand, and the problematic nature of that desire, on the other. Here, his complaint was not simply with the conservative traditions of high modernism but with avant-gardism as well—which may have hardened into its own limiting tradition. So, with *Ghostcatching* (a 1999 digital video installation), Jones invoked formalism (via digital technology) but then contextualized it by moments of live improvisation as a guilty pleasure or privilege that he could not quite indulge or condone. Eddie Torres also grappled with the consequences of broad appeal. An acclaimed mambo dancer at the Palladium as a teenager, Torres decided later in life to formalize his technique and teach it to the general public by offering studio classes. Yet, in retrospect, he wondered whether this formalization and increased legibility hampered his ability to improvise, thus lessening the critical force of his dancing.

Although these tensions are important to recognize, the question of legibility is nevertheless in some ways peripheral to my discussion of politics. I am not claiming that improvisation's keenest power exists as a result of its message or in the breadth of its effect. Instead, this book explores improvised dance as a vital technology of the self—an ongoing, critical, physical, and anticipatory readiness that, while grounded in the individual, is necessary for a vibrant sociality and vital civil society. My primary concern is with the experiences that improvised practice offers the dancer, even though I do also believe that the social landscape has the potential to shift as a result of dancers' improvised engagement with constraint. As I argue in my final chapter, in certain rare instances, improvisers create thrilling new spaces in which to dance.

Mambo's Open Shines: Causing Circles at the Palladium

The book's first chapter, "Mambo's Open Shines," looks at New York's Palladium ballroom during the mid-1950s, focusing on the dynamic breaks where couples split apart to dance solo improvisations, poetically known as "open shines." The Palladium's racial integration was unique for its time, and the dance hall provided a place where people left behind the disappointments of everyday life to dance and be glamorous, if only for a few hours. Still, the Palladium was not a "free" space where everything was equal and anything was possible. A variety of constraints, imposed by racism, sexism, and physical training, shaped how people moved within the Palladium on any given night. The chapter discusses these social constraints, as well as mambo's unique rhythmic and choreographic structures, which, I argue, constituted different but related kinds of tight places that dancers negotiated with particular brilliance. The chapter ultimately argues that the moments of resistance that occurred as dancers improvised at the Palladium, while meaningful in many ways, were neither shared by nor identical for the dance hall's many patrons.

Mambo frames my study of improvised dance precisely because it challenges the origin myths that dominate published dance histories. Much of the improvised work presented on New York concert stages during the 1960s and 1970s had its seeds in dance halls such as the Palladium, where dancers honed their skills at improvisational principles like breaking and investigated complex relationships with music. But to say that postmodern dance "has seeds" in improvised social dance is not to claim a clear beginning. When one looks to mambo's development in Cuba, it becomes clear that it emerged with influences from many places. My opening chapter sketches the various European and African traditions that contributed to the formation of mambo in

Cuba before going on to analyze how the circulation of movies and records, as well as the movement of actual people, enabled it to travel across borders. Having developed in multiple directions, with rich midcentury convergences among Cuban, Puerto Rican, and African American musicians and dancers, mambo demands a dynamic consideration of improvisation's relation to traditions of black expressive culture. Mambo immediately challenges the tendency to reduce blackness to the African American male, a point that remains important throughout the book.

My discussion of mambo also complicates divisions between "high" and "low" forms of dance and the tendency to reduce forms of social dance to easy entertainment, generally legible and immediately accessible. Many of the dancers at the Palladium ballroom during the 1950s were responding to societal tight places created by poverty, racism, and sexism that would have been recognizable to most onlookers regardless of their dance literacy. Moreover, as suggested by the term *social dance,* mambo was popular among the masses and attracted far more public interest than the other improvisational performances discussed in the book. People flocked to the Palladium to participate in the dancing, as well as to watch the greats who competed and showcased their tremendous skill on the dance floor. People moved between doing and watching at the Palladium. But to emphasize the social nature of mambo is not to suggest that it was ahistorical or any less experimental than, say, contact improvisation or the Judson Dance Theater. All too often scholars reduce social dance to a simple expression of lived experience, rather than a historically grounded aesthetic craft. In fact, many of the dancers at the Palladium were the very same dancers who appeared on concert stages and vice versa, an important example being Katherine Dunham, whose studio was a place where dancers came to train for work in a range of venues. Robert Farris Thompson explains:

> What was happening on the dance floor was critical and revolutionary: demolition of the conviction that only in ballet do we have an art history. . . . In truth New York mambo comprised a complex interaction of known personalities [such as Dotty Adams, Millie Donay, Ernie Ensley, and Anibal Vázquez] out of which a classic style emerged. Palladium art history was *not* anonymous. It reflected conscious choices, by named creative women and named creative men, interacting with further conscious choices by other named creative people—dancers, musicians, and singers, all equal in the creative process.[78]

Mambo at the Palladium was experimental. It was historical. It was relational. It was complex. And it required training. Why else would the dance hall have employed instructors to give lessons early in the evenings? As with any art, one can experience dance on many different levels. But to catch the references, the structure, or the rhythmic play of an improvisation on the Palladium dance floor (particularly by those dancers who would compete or gather in the ballroom's southwest corner, designated for the most avid improvisers), an observer required a sensitive eye and a well-developed sense of context.

We Insist! Seeing Music and Hearing Dance

The book's second chapter considers collaborations between postmodern dancers and free jazz musicians during the late 1960s and early 1970s, showing some of the explicit ways that dance hall innovations such as improvised "breaks" and communication across genres influenced experimentation within New York's avant-garde dance scene. The chapter begins with a discussion of collaborations between Judith Dunn and Bill Dixon. Dunn danced with the Merce Cunningham Dance Company for five years and was an instrumental member of the Judson Dance Theater. Bill Dixon is a trumpeter, visual artist, and founder of the Black Music Division at Bennington College. In addition to creating striking improvised works, their collaborations explored and openly acknowledged relations between what has been deemed a black, masculine tradition of improvised music and the rather white, feminine world of postmodern dance. Their visions of artistic freedom (which, I argue, were never separate from the social world in which they lived) often differed, yet Dunn and Dixon explored those differences through rigorous improvisational practice.

The chapter also discusses the work of Dianne McIntyre, a dancer who further challenged the racial and gender divisions within the worlds of improvised music and dance. In many ways, McIntyre received the same modernist training as Dunn. But as a black woman, she fit into the tradition differently. McIntyre worked with a number of musicians throughout her career, including Cecil Taylor, Olu Dara, Butch Morris, and Abbey Lincoln. She also studied with dancers from Harlem's Savoy ballroom, demonstrating yet again the deep relations between the midcentury dance hall and the concert stage. Influenced by the civil rights era and the Black Arts Movement, in

1972 McIntyre formed an ensemble of improvising musicians and dancers called Sounds in Motion. Through working with free jazz musicians, McIntyre realized that improvised music and dance are both deeply corporeal, a discovery with tremendous political implications. Once one recognizes the embodied nature of both art forms, it becomes difficult to elevate music as a masculine art of the mind over the bodily art of dance.

The work of Dunn, Dixon, and McIntyre emerged out of an urgent historical moment and demanded a new kind of engagement from its audience. For this reason, the end of the chapter moves to a discussion of ethical audience reception. How might one approach this body of improvised work, which involves movement but also sound, without reducing its complexity or silencing its politics? I argue that the complexity of Sounds in Motion's work demands that one move beyond isolated modes of viewing dance and hearing music. Instead, one must engage an "ensemble of the senses."[79] One also must consider the social and historical context in which these improvisational performances took place.

Bodies on the Line: Contact Improvisation and Techniques of Nonviolent Protest

Moving from *The Freedom Now Suite* to the 1961 Freedom Rides, the third chapter analyzes contact improvisation and its relation to the corporeality of protest. Contact improvisation was a partnered form of improvised dance that rejected traditional hierarchies in Western concert dance during the 1970s. Rather than focus on contact improvisation's democratic ideals, however, as many scholars have done, I analyze contact improvisation as an embodied practice of self-readiness. Unlike their modernist forbears, contact improvisers investigated stillness and sought ways to improvise in the midst of unfamiliar falls. By doing this, they widened the range of physical possibility within the realm of concert dance and found ways to make choices and maintain physical safety in moments of duress. In this way, the training that contact improvisers developed resembles techniques of nonviolent protest used in the civil rights movement by organizations such as the Congress On Racial Equality (CORE).

This, of course, is a fraught comparison since contact improvisation's development occurred in the safety of lofts and gymnasiums, and most of its practitioners were white. The stakes were significant in both instances, but of nowhere near the same magnitude. And so this chapter tries to accomplish several things. On the one hand, I want to argue that contact improvisation offered a physical practice in which dancers readied themselves for a range of possible situations. This is where it seems to me the political potential of contact improvisation exists most strongly, and it is where the practice intersects with radical techniques of nonviolent protest. On the other hand, the chapter holds on to the important point that one must consider the conditions and contexts in which any physical practice occurs.

The Breathing Show: *Improvisation in the Work of Bill T. Jones*

The fourth chapter discusses the significance of improvisation across Bill T. Jones's career, from his rejection of contact improvisation, to his identity-driven works, to his controversial return to formalism. The importance of improvisation for Jones becomes particularly salient in *The Breathing Show,* an evening of solo performance made in the twilight of his performing career. Jones began to work on *The Breathing Show* in 1998, when, at the age of forty-six, he found himself both embroiled in controversy due to his renewed interest in form and concerned about his legacy. The more he worked on the evening-length performance, the more important improvisation became. According to Jones, "It's curious and unsettling, but I feel *The Breathing Show* only began to come alive when I decided to speak and to allow myself to improvise."[80]

In order to discuss how exactly improvisation "enlivened" *The Breathing Show,* I will analyze the relationship between Jones's onstage presence and *Ghostcatching,* an installation that used motion-capture technology to present traces of Jones's prior improvisations. With *Ghostcatching,* the improvisations became virtual, moving in a sense *beyond* the body. How then, if at all, does the work hold onto its politics? Does *Ghostcatching* represent Jones's most radical formalist turn? Can politics transpire in a virtual dance that allows neither sweat nor skin, primary markers of labor and race, to appear on stage? Complicating current discussions of Jones's renewed interest in form, I will place *Ghostcatching* within a history of imaging technologies, tracing how the dancing body intersects with technology, labor, and race. Ultimately, I suggest that by juxtaposing *Ghostcatching* and live improvisations, Jones enabled politics and a critical perspective on issues of identity to emerge, even through the skinless medium of digital technology.

Exquisite Dancing: Altering the Terrain of Tight Places

The examples of improvised dance analyzed throughout the book enable a critical discussion of physical techniques; the effects of material, social, and historical conditions on one's dancing; and the increasingly complex relation between improvised dance and documentation. By analyzing each example as a series of unique interactions with constraint, the book challenges the facile way in which dance studies pairs improvised dance with freedom.

Of course, it may seem strange that a study so bent on analyzing improvisation's relation to various types of constraint can purport to be about freedom in any positive sense. In the conclusion, drawing from Michel Foucault's late interviews, I analyze the extent to which improvised dance can be considered a "practice of freedom."[81] I also reflect upon the exquisite moments of dancing that erupt throughout the book. These striking moments demonstrate that tight places need not be equated with impermeable limits. As Foucault maintains in an interview conducted just months before his death, "One cannot impute to me the idea that power is a system of domination which controls everything and leaves no room for freedom."[82] Likewise, a call for greater attention to "tight places" is in no way to deny improvisation's political potential. If anything, it is the sped-up, imaginative, expressive negotiation with *constraint* that defines improvisation. To imagine it any other way is not only to deny the real conditions in which we find ourselves but also to deny improvisation its keenest political power as a vital technology of the self.

CHAPTER 1 *Mambo's Open Shines: Causing Circles at the Palladium*

Mura Dehn's *The Spirit Moves,* a three-part film of social dance from 1900 through the 1950s, offers a rare opportunity to see the mambo dancing that flourished in midcentury New York City. In grainy black and white, the film contains two types of mambo footage: scenes of masses dancing at the Palladium and the Savoy, two famous New York City ballrooms, and more carefully staged improvisations that Dehn recorded in a studio. In the film's dance hall scenes, people gather in crowded spaces to watch the evening's most exceptional dancers. The spectators look on with rapt attention, occasionally swaying or shifting in response to musical breaks. Meanwhile, dressed for a night on the town, the dancers weave in and out of each other's spaces, spinning intricate mambos on a packed wooden floor.

With mambo, couples alternate between partnered embraces and solo improvisations poetically known as "open shines." Several couples in Dehn's film display stunning improvisational skill, but one couple's stealthy rhythmic sensibility quickly focuses our attention: a long-limbed man, clad in a pale suit and dark tie, and a woman with cropped hair, wearing a shiny tank dress and open-toe, high-heeled shoes. Delicately touching the man's left hand, the woman circles counterclockwise, taking small steps, punctuating the *clave* with a regular 2/4 beat. Meanwhile, her hips swing side to side, flesh pressing against satin in an aching rubato. She slaps her left thigh repeatedly as her partner moves on the musical downbeat, carving his own concentric circles as he slowly descends toward the ground.

Elsewhere on the dance floor, two partners circle widely around each other. The man stops repeatedly during the course of his open shine, halting expansively before reentering the music's rhythmic pulse. At one point, he executes a whirling inward turn on one leg, breaking with his back arched. Time freezes. And then he languidly pitches forward to pick up where he left off. Meanwhile, his partner circles around him, purse clutched in her raised left hand. She takes small steps, forward and back, projecting awareness from every surface of her body. Surveying the scene, she inscribes a delicate moat around herself as she goes. But with impeccable smoothness, she rejoins her partner, and they continue their mambo with arms intertwined.

In addition to the dance hall footage described earlier, *The Spirit Moves* contains more carefully staged improvisations that Dehn filmed in a studio. As in the dance hall scenes, Dehn's studio footage reveals virtuosic improvisations. But in the studio, the walls and floor are covered entirely in white, suggesting an attempt to render the room "neutral," so one can focus on the dancing. No space, however, is ever neutral, and no dancing occurs in a vacuum. Ngugi wa Thiong'o makes this point in his response to Peter Brook's famous pronouncement that any empty space could be a bare stage. According to wa Thiong'o: "Performance space is never empty. Bare, yes; open, yes; but never empty. It is always the site of physical, social, and psychic forces in society."[1] Obviously, the dancers in Dehn's studio scenes were dancing in a particular time and place—in a studio in the 1950s, in front of Mura Dehn, a Russian woman who had studied at the Moscow Art Theatre and the Academy of Arts in Vienna and became fascinated by jazz and black social dance upon moving to the United States. What's disturbing is that the whiteness of the studio suggests an attempt to erase context. One cannot distinguish floor from walls from ceiling. The dancers, in this case mostly people of color, appear in a created "nowhere," fetishized in a freaky, floating world.

Although it is unlikely that this was Dehn's intention, the juxtaposition of studio and dance hall scenes in *The Spirit Moves* emphasizes the importance of context when considering the political significance of mambo. What's at stake when a woman spontaneously clutches her purse above her head, while taking small steps and surveying the scene? What does it mean to emphasize a musical break, choosing when and how to move again? What's significant about a white Russian woman, camera in hand, who is utterly fascinated by black social dance in New York City? One cannot remove dance from its social and historical contexts and expect to understand its political meaning. This chapter's discussion of mambo therefore focuses on a particular time and location: mambo as it was danced in the mid-1950s at the Palladium ball-

room, an extravagant dance hall located in midtown Manhattan on the corner of Broadway and 53rd Street.

The Palladium's racial integration was unique for its time, enabling many
people to step away from their everyday lives to dance and be glamorous for
a few hours. Reflecting on their evenings at the Palladium, dancers frequently
explain in golden terms how they were transformed and greatly moved by
their experience. But the Palladium was not a "free" space where everything
was equal and anything was possible. A variety of constraints, imposed by
racism, sexism, and physical training, shaped how people moved within the
Palladium on any given night. Although people engaged with social norms
and expectations in multiple locations—as they ordered drinks, or walked up
the stairs, or paid their admission fees—these negotiations achieved particular brilliance on the dance floor, especially in mambo's improvised breaks.

As partners split apart to dance solo improvisations—with elegant circles
and swinging hips—they negotiated the social strictures of the space in both
rhythmic and choreographic terms. The results were neither uniform nor
guaranteed, but that is what made the improvisations most powerful and urgently live. For the most skilled improvisers, the Palladium was not a place in
which constraint could be completely or straightforwardly ignored. On the
contrary, dancers became intimately acquainted with a shifting landscape of
tight places, rigorously exploring its contours. Night after night, they moved
their bodies in relation to those strictures, testing limits and creating fleeting
new spaces in which to shine.

Traversing Borders

Scholars typically begin their histories of mambo by describing a variety of
charged scenes. Robert Farris Thompson begins his particular tale in Havana, 1939, with a dramatic incident emphasizing the presence of Kongo re-
ligion in mambo. As Thompson tells the story, Orestes López, a composer
and instrumentalist who guided one of Cuba's most prominent *danzón* orchestras, introduced the religious term *mambo* into the dance hall. López believed that singing the word *mambo* from a bandstand had the potential to
inspire vivid reactions.[2] As he predicted, chants of "Mambo! Mambo!"
transformed into deep, staccato orchestral syncopation. On the dance floor,
couples spontaneously split apart to dance, with men circling women and
women circling men. According to Thompson, this dance hall event had

tremendous implications, splitting the Western couple dance and introducing African forms and religious feeling into symphonic music.[3]

In telling the story of Orestes López, Thompson describes a significant evening that possibly instigated the naming of dance hall mambo. But the deep African presence in the dance did not emerge on account of an individual's singular inspiration, on a particular night. Yvonne Daniel's careful study "Cuban Dance: An Orchard of Caribbean Creativity" sketches the various European and African antecedents that contributed to the formation of mambo. Daniel begins by discussing the European influences within Cuban dance culture, which came from southern Spain but also from French colonists who left Haiti for Cuba around the time of the Haitian revolution at the beginning of the nineteenth century. She explains that the European seeds within Cuban dance contributed "straight back posture, touching of male and female partners, stanza with verse song-style, and interest in rhythm (seen in stamped foot patterns and some hip movement)."[4] Interestingly, Daniel attributes this early emphasis on the hips to the presence of North African culture that existed within Spain from the Moors' invasion, beginning in the eighth century. Revealing the complex ways in which movement travels across borders and cultures, and highlighting the problem with simple origin stories, Daniel suggests that early African traces within Cuban dances came from within Europe.[5]

The later African influence came as Africans from the coasts of West and Central Africa were brought to Cuba as an enslaved labor force to aid in sugar production. Daniel claims that, out of the many African ethnic groups brought to Cuba, four distinct dance and music traditions emerged into prominence: "(1) *Kongo* (or *Kongo-Angolan, Bantú,* or *Palo*), (2) *Arará,* (3) *Carabalí* (*Abakuá* or *Ñáñigo*), and the best known, (4) *Yoruba* (or *Lucumí, Oricha,* or *Santería*)."[6] Although significant differences exist among these traditions, Cuban dance forms have been influenced greatly by their similarities, most notably an emphasis on polyrhythm, played on percussion instruments as well as danced with isolated body parts; a call-and-response pattern between singer and chorus; accentuated use of the lower body, with dynamic hip movement; and, of course, improvisation.[7]

During the mid-nineteenth century, several uniquely Cuban dance forms emerged out of the diverse movement traditions that made their way onto Cuban soil. Daniel outlines five major developments: *el son, la rumba, el danzón, el punto guajiro o campesino,* and *la canción cubana,* a song-form that is not danced. According to Daniel, one can see blended variations of European and African cultures in *son,* which is danced to a rhythm called *son clave*—a syncopated rhythmic pattern that repeats as either "one, two / one, two, three //" or "one, two, three / one, two //." This rhythmic pattern exists throughout Cuba's African-derived traditions and in various musical traditions with African roots across the Caribbean and North America. Musicians in Cuba initially played *sones* with Spanish guitars, but the form expanded to include African drums, woodwind instruments, and even pianos. As for the dance, couples touch in a European manner, with relatively straight backs. But the dance accentuates the hips, allowing a division between the upper and lower torso, which creates visible polyrhythms within the body. All of this takes place over an intricate, rhythmic foot pattern.

Mambo emerged in the 1940s and 1950s as one of *son*'s most popular international variations, traversing numerous borders. Travel, immigration, and the circulation of movies and records resulted in mambo's wide dispersion and caused changes in its form and significance. Daniel provides an excellent description of mambo, noting differences between Cuban and New York styles during the 1940s and 1950s. According to Daniel, the Cuban mambo had a bouncy quality, with a "touch, step" foot pattern alternating between the right and left foot. She writes: "The toe of the right foot touches the floor momentarily and then the whole right foot takes a step; this pattern is repeated on the left and continues to alternate. Above, the hips (really pelvis) move forward and back with each touch, step of the feet. The hands and arms move alternately forward and back, each arm in opposition to the feet."[8] Daniel explains that outside of Cuba, particularly in New York, mambo retained a "short, short, long" foot pattern along with "the suave and seductive sense of its earlier son heritage."[9] In Cuba and elsewhere, partners engaged in a series of partnered turns, and in the United States, couples broke from the closed partner stance to improvise separately in open shines before rejoining in a closed-partner position. This was the Palladium dancers' claim to fame, and it was where dancers tried most to develop individual style.

Dancers in Cuba danced mambo throughout the 1940s, as a variety of composers, including Arsenio Rodríguez and Dámaso Pérez Prado, transcribed Orestes López's orchestral innovations. Then, by the early 1950s, the recording industry helped to instigate the musical form's global popularity. When Prado moved to Mexico City in 1949, he frequented one of RCA Victor's studios and recorded hugely popular mambo renditions that were played on radios and sold internationally.[10]

Of course, a desire for Cuban music within the United States had been growing well before mambo became popular, with executives from record companies making regular trips to Cuba as early as 1890 in search of promising performers. The fascination with Latin music and dance then grew markedly during the era of Franklin Roosevelt's "Good Neighbor Policy." In the president's inaugural address in 1933, signaling what he said was his desire to improve relations with Central and South America and to distance the United States from past interventionist policies, Roosevelt pronounced, "In the field of world policy I would dedicate this nation to the policy of the good neighbor—the neighbor who resolutely respects himself and, because he does so, respects the rights of others."[11] As part of Roosevelt's opposition to armed intervention, he abolished the 1903 treaty with Cuba that granted the United States the power to intervene militarily in Cuban affairs in order to "preserve [its] internal stability or independence."[12]

The "Good Neighbor Policy" had a cultural arm as well, with the State Department suggesting that Hollywood might breach the cultural divide between the United States and Latin America. Although its aim was to eradicate racist stereotypes and cultural bias, the "Latin explosion" in cinema hardly succeeded on these terms. In "Of Rhythms and Borders," Ana López discusses portrayals of Latin American music and dance in classic Hollywood cinema. She argues that Hollywood's fetishistic interest in "all things Latin" presented utter disregard for national specificity. To illustrate this point, she notes:

> Carmen Miranda is incongruously "Brazilian" in a studio-produced Argentina (*Down Argentine Way*, Irving Cummings, 1940) and Cuba (*Weekend in Havana*, Walter Lang, 1941); Desi Arnaz [plays] an Argentine conga-playing student in New Mexico college in *Too Many Girls* (George Abbott, 1940); Ricardo Montalbán [plays] a Mexican classical composer that dances Spanish flamenco in *Fiesta* (Jack Cummings, 1947); and Gene Kelly [plays] an Anglo sailor on leave who happens upon a stage version of *Olvera Street* in the Los Angeles of *Anchors Aweigh* (Stanley Donen, 1945) and dances a "Mexican Hat Dance" to the Argentine tango "La cumparsita."[13]

Classic Hollywood films frequently mangled cultural specificity in their representations of cultural others. Still, one must be careful that analyses of appropriation don't obscure other complex modes of exchange and reception.

For example, careful study of mambo suggests that a one-directional story of pure subaltern origin followed by hegemonic appropriation is too simple. As illustrated in Daniel's complex genealogy of music and dance traditions in Cuba, where dance forms like *son* are already deep amalgamations, one can't say that mambo originated in Cuba and then moved directly to Hollywood, where it was monolithically appropriated and Anglicized. While appropriation did occur, seen not only in movies but in dance studios where upright versions of "Latin" dances with minimal syncopation and virtually no improvisation were taught, mambo's movement, especially in the early to mid-1950s, was complicated and multidirectional.

In discussing the importance of cinema in mambo's rise to popularity, Thompson makes the interesting point that all-black films in the 1940s, such as *Cabin in the Sky* and *Stormy Weather,* affected mambo in Cuba, where dancers began to incorporate moves like lindy swing-outs and spins over rumba's pelvic movement.[14] These two MGM films from 1943 contained several dance scenes performed by phenomenal dancers such as Leon James, John Bubbles, Archie Savage, Bill Robinson, and Katherine Dunham. Although *Stormy Weather* tells the story of a World War I vet (Robinson) who falls in love with a singer (Lena Horne) and decides to go into show business, the plot primarily provides a showcase for Robinson's legendary tapping, both light and incredibly clear. Robinson tapped high on his toes, with an upper body that remained upright and swinging. Although one could argue that black representations in these films were stereotypical—a group of happy-go-lucky entertainers—Thompson's observation shows several things: that mambo changed in Cuba as well as in the United States and that, as Jane Desmond notes, "appropriation does not always take the form of the hegemonic group's 'borrowing' from subordinated groups."[15] Perhaps more important, Thompson points to a deep exchange between Cuban and African American expressive cultures that took place in both Cuba and the United States.

Katherine Dunham, an African American choreographer and anthropologist who conducted fieldwork in Cuba, Jamaica, Martinique, Trinidad, and Haiti, furthered this type of exchange and greatly influenced the development of New York mambo. Having danced since early childhood, she attended the University of Chicago to study "not only how people dance but, even more importantly, why they dance as they do."[16] Dunham confounded people by inhabiting the roles of both dancer and scholar. Reflecting on these dual roles in 1941, she explained: "In the great raft of publicity which, in the past few months, has appeared in connection with my role in the Broadway show *Cabin in the Sky,* I find myself referred to, and on the very same day, both as 'the hottest thing on Broadway' and 'an intelligent, sensitive young woman . . . an anthropologist of note.' Personally, I do not think of myself as either one of these extreme phenomena. But reporters, confronted by the simultaneous presence of two such diverse elements, have often failed to grasp the synthesis between them."[17]

Perhaps most interesting for this chapter's discussion of mambo is the fact that Dunham not only traveled across national borders as part of her fieldwork but also moved with great agility among the worlds of ritual, the dance hall, and the concert stage—and fostered that kind of movement among others. Susan Manning has argued that Dunham helped to make the performance of diaspora legible to white critics in the early 1940s by choreographing dances based on Latin American and Caribbean sources, as well as nineteenth-century African American dances deriving from minstrelsy and plantations and later twentieth-century jazz dancing.[18] Vanoye Aikens, who danced with the Dunham company from 1943 to 1965, recalls: "No one had collected Caribbean and Latin material and presented it in the theater the way that Katherine Dunham did. No one had ever thought of Voodooism without thinking of something kinky before Katherine Dunham. No one had ever seen a trained company in folkloric material re-choreographed without any of the ethnic qualities taken away and presented on stage with trained dancers. And that is what Katherine Dunham did."[19]

But Dunham did more than place the fruits of her fieldwork on the stage. She frequented jazz clubs and dance halls throughout her time in New York City, places that profoundly influenced the already rich and complicated exchanges among Caribbean, Latino, and African American expressive cultures. As Joyce Aschenbrenner notes:

> Dunham brought an appreciation of the origins of Latin rhythms in African religions to audiences in the Latino community in New York, as well as elsewhere. Her staging of the dances, displaying the cultural context, influenced Cubans and other Latinos to make their own artistic presentations. Recordings of Latin rhythms by Tito Puente and Chano Pozo acquainted North Americans with the vitality of the Cuban beat. Pozo, who was a drummer in the Dunham Company, played with Dizzy Gillespie's band, introducing Latin rhythms into jazz. Other Cuban drummers

in the company included Francisco Aguabella and Albert Laguerre, and Gilberto Valdés, "a brilliant young composer and conductor," [who] wrote music based on Afro-Cuban themes for the company.[20]

In addition to employing talented Afro-Cuban drummers in her professional company, Dunham operated a school from 1945 to 1957 on 43rd Street and Broadway, just ten blocks south of the Palladium. Initially offering courses in dance, speech, and various theater techniques, the school expanded into the Katherine Dunham School of Cultural Arts in 1952, providing a fertile meeting ground where dancers and musicians could mingle and learn from one another. Dunham hosted Prado and the famous Palladium drummer Tito Puente at some of the school's monthly gatherings. Meanwhile, Palladium dancers such as Millie Donay and Pedro Aguilar studied at the school, which offered a holistic curriculum including dance and theater, but also courses in languages, anthropology, sociology, and psychology. Instructors ranged from the choreographer José Limón to the anthropologist Margaret Mead.

Fostering traffic among the dance hall, the studio, and the stage, the Dunham School provided a meaningful avenue through which African religious movements made their way onto the Palladium's dance floor. As Dunham wrote in "Thesis Turned Broadway," "Certainly the great sweep of Latin American dances brings with it choreographic patterns rich in African and Creole African lore."[21] Referring to a rattling of the head that frequently appeared at the Palladium and that closely resembled head movements by possessed women in Agogo, Ghana, Thompson explains, "The mamboists have a theory as to how it came to New York: it stems from Katherine Dunham's incomparable knowledge, of motion and dance in Africa, entering mambo when several Palladium dancers studied with her in the 1950s to deepen their fluency in blackness."[22] According to Thompson, the variety of styles present in New York mambo emerged as a "logical consequence of colliding mainland black and Caribbean modes of motion."[23]

Thompson's claim that African American dancers studied with Katherine Dunham to better understand their own blackness suggests that the collisions between mainland black and Caribbean ways of moving weren't merely the result of happenstance. In *Between Race and Empire: African-Americans and Cubans before the Cuban Revolution,* the editors Lisa Brock and Digna Castañeda Fuertes present a collection of essays that uncovers some of the many unrecognized but deeply significant linkages between African American and Cuban forms of expressive culture.[24] According to Brock, many Cuban artists found solace and an enlivened race consciousness in Harlem during the 1940s and 1950s. For example, when asked during a visit to Cuba in the 1940s if he intended to remain in Cuba, musician Mario Bauzá explained: "I only got one plan. I want to be with people like me [in the United States, to] know what it is to be a black man in a black [country]. My roots have got to be there. [There, in Harlem,] was a big black race, they had shows, they had good orchestras, good artists."[25] In keeping with Bauzá's sentiments, Brock claims that the arts were central in the solidarity expressed between Afro-Cubans and African Americans, with meaningful contact established at late-night studios, neighborhood restaurants, baseball diamonds, nightclubs, and dance halls. Brock explains, "While rarely articulated as overt political ideology or as a response to empire, these activities in fact were. Afro-Cubans and African-Americans spoke with their ears, their eyes, their entire bodies, their cheers, and most importantly their desires; they entered into each other's music and reveled in each other's athletic prowess."[26] She claims that their cultural expressions—for example, their music and dance—"shared similar African roots and served parallel counterhegemonic functions."[27] These shared aesthetics and modes of creation, which were sites for ideological contestation and political assertion, attracted Afro-Cubans and African Americans to each other.

Brock also argues that of all the retentions that exist within the African diaspora, "the art of improvisation has been particularly thrilling to both audiences and performers."[28] But why exactly was improvisation so thrilling to both African American and Latino/a dancers in midcentury New York? In "Rebellions of Everynight Life," Celeste Fraser Delgado and José Muñoz claim that Africanist retentions such as improvisation sustain subalterns who otherwise lack cultural and historical capital.[29] According to Delgado and Muñoz, improvisation is crucial in nightlife's danced "rebellions" because it escapes forces of commercialization and fetishization. Moreover, they argue that improvisation's flexibility enables dancers to negotiate their relations to their cultural pasts as well as to the present. They explain, "Improvisation links cultural memory to the here and now, where the meaning of the dance is continually renewed to the (poly)rhythms of history in force in the present."[30]

Delgado and Muñoz recognize that the fluidity of improvisation offers dancers the opportunity to make choices and constantly renew their dances.

However, they also claim that "the dancing body not only assures survival of cultural memory of the past, but the dances of resistance assure survival of the dancers in the present tense."[31] While empowering on the surface, the first part of this claim is too grand. Improvisation's necessary openness—the very thing that allows dancers to make spontaneous choices as they negotiate their positions between a shifting past and present—also denies the "assurance" that cultural memory will survive.

While Mura Dehn observed Africanist retentions on the Palladium's dance floor, she noted that many of the young New York dancers had no knowledge of their motions' relation to African rituals. Some Palladium dancers had grown up with an understanding of traditional African influences, while others had gained this understanding at places like the Dunham School. But some dancers developed their movements far more haphazardly on the dance floor, picking their moves for a host of reasons, ranging from aesthetic criteria to a vague sense of pleasure. Recalling the arm movements of a Puerto Rican dancer, Dehn explains: "They had a quality of 'Egugu,' shown to me by a Nigerian dance master and drummer. 'This dance,' he said, 'came from a sacred ritual of death and resurrection. The movements have significance like the sign of the cross has for us.'"[32] Still, according to Dehn, although the young Puerto Rican moved his arms with great fluidity, he had no understanding of the motion's varied meanings. For him, the arm movements were merely ornamental.

Dancers encountered a variety of movement styles on the Palladium's dance floor, and the improvisational space of open shines demanded that these dancers figure out how to move in relation to a host of influences. Puente used to say that he loved playing at the Palladium because he could look out from the bandstand and see a bit of everything on the dance floor.[33] Similarly, Eddie Torres, who frequented the Palladium as a teenager, explains that at an integrated, multinational dance hall like the Palladium, "people started to realize that mambo offered that real area of improv where any movement from any form of dance could be expressed."[34] This "area of improv" is significant, as it places a different set of demands on the dancer than choreography. When one learns a sequence of choreography, one learns a series of movements that unfold in a set rhythm. Although dancers undoubtedly make interpretive choices when performing choreography, there is no "next move" ready and waiting in improvised social dance. Improvisation presents an elastic relation to constraint, which demands that the dancer ac-

tively participate in determining how a given dance will unfold. This demand
for participation is particularly important because one must do more than assume an imitative position or relax in the belief that one is separate from the
dance's development.

With improvised social dance, one must contribute to ▮▮▮▮▮▮▮▮▮▮▮▮
be implicated in the movement one generates. Such dancing ▮▮▮▮▮▮▮▮▮▮▮
at a place like the Palladium, where dancers encountered a variety of dance
styles and rhythms, as well as the social preconceptions and norms that course
through any public space. With each passing moment, dancers faced a host of
decisions: Shall I move my arms in a manner that, for some, has deep ritualis-
tic significance? Shall I keep my back vertical like a ballroom dancer? Shall I
shimmy my shoulders like a showgirl? Shall I introduce aerial moves like the
African American dancers who developed the lindy hop? Although it is unlikely that dancers actually form such questions in language while in the midst
of improvising, they no doubt feel the rewards or consequences of making one
choice versus another, especially in a public dance hall where spectators
abound. Faced with an array of possible movements, each one laden with layers of social meaning, there is no guarantee that cultural memory will survive.
Nor is present-tense survival guaranteed. This instability, however, is what
makes improvisation most meaningful, with negotiations both ongoing and
urgently live. These negotiations occurred on a nightly basis in New York's
Palladium ballroom, where people with different memories, cultural affilia-
tions, and dancing experience converged in unprecedented ways.

Dancing in a Very Full Space

Located on the corner of Broadway and 53rd Street in Manhattan, the Palladium had previously been occupied by the Dreamland Dancing Academy, a
swing club that lost its liquor license in 1944 after the arrest of two dance
hostesses on prostitution charges. Two years later, Louis Levine, Sylvia Cole,
and Hyman Sigel filed papers to become incorporated as the Palladium Ballroom, which remained open for business from 1947 to 1966. In the early days,
the Palladium suffered financially, as did many ballrooms during the 1940s.
According to Vernon Boggs, although swing bands were tremendously popular from the 1920s to the 1940s, New York's dancing nightlife suffered as
cabaret licenses became more restrictive and the jazz world embraced bebop,
an avant-garde music considered less conducive to dancing than swing.[35]

Attempting to bring more business to the Palladium, the ballroom's manager, Tommy Morton, sought out the Cuban musicians Frank "Machito" Grillo and Mario Bauzá for advice. Bauzá had come to the United States in 1930, becoming Chick Webb's lead trumpeter in 1933 and joining Cab Calloway in 1939. Bauzá stayed with Calloway for a year but then formed his own band in 1940, along with Machito, his brother-in-law. The band was called Machito's Afro-Cubans, a name whose embrace of African heritage was radical for its time and place.[36] Machito and Bauzá, who played in both Cuba and New York City, learned a lot about jazz through their Harlem gigs and pulled from both strands of music as Afro-Cuban jazz grew in popularity throughout the 1940s.[37] In an encounter frequently repeated in histories of the Palladium, Morton asked Machito and Bauzá how to increase the Palladium's success. Once Morton admitted that "the only color he cared about was green," meaning that money trumped race in his business decisions, the two musicians suggested that Morton speak with Federico Pagani.

"El Gran Federico," as Pagani was commonly called, was a small Puerto Rican man who had moved with his family in 1925 from San Juan to New York's El Barrio, a neighborhood in East Harlem that was then primarily Jewish and Italian but soon became home to many of the Puerto Ricans who moved to New York after being granted U.S. citizenship in 1917. An avid trumpeter, Pagani switched in 1940 from playing to promoting Latin music and dance.[38] When approached by the Palladium's manager in 1947, Pagani suggested that the ballroom move carefully with its new integration, first forming a Sunday matinee for Latin music. The group in charge of organizing the Sunday dance parties became the Blen Blen Club, named after a composition by the Afro-Cuban *conguero* Chano Pozo. Pagani went to work, handing out flyers throughout Harlem, and the first Sunday matinee was an unprecedented success. Six bands played at the matinee, which lasted from two P.M. until nine P.M., packing the dance hall to maximum capacity. Lines of people circled the block, and the police, fearing riots, shut down local traffic. In a single afternoon, the Blen Blen Club brought more money into the Palladium than the dance hall had earned since opening.[39] Within a few weeks, the Palladium extended the Sunday-afternoon offerings to Wednesday evenings, and before the end of the year, the dance hall dedicated itself entirely to a burgeoning music in New York: Afro-Cuban jazz.[40]

By the early 1950s, the Palladium ballroom had become one of the most important Latin dance clubs in New York City, with numerous dance halls such as Harlem's Savoy Ballroom instigating "mambo nights" in an effort to duplicate the Palladium's success. During this time, two Puerto Rican musicians, Ernesto "Tito" Puente and Pablo "Tito" Rodríguez—Puente born in East Harlem and Rodríguez in Santurce, Puerto Rico—joined Machito's band in playing regularly at the packed-to-capacity Palladium. Before long, however, a rivalry developed among the Palladium's three in-house bands, each fighting for top marquee billing. People typically describe Machito as the respected elder statesman, Tito Rodríguez as the romantic, impeccably dressed balladeer, and Tito Puente as the more rumpled but amazing arranger and percussionist.[41] Competition pushed the nightly performance energy and musical innovation.

According to Vernon Boggs, in addition to the brilliant music, two factors contributed to the Palladium's success: the public's desire to dance again after the demise of big-band swing and the significant increase in New York's Cuban and Puerto Rican populations. But the Palladium was also appealing because it possessed an atmosphere full of grandeur. Mura Dehn famously pronounced the Palladium "the most glamorous popular dance hall in New York."[42] Surrounded by the glittering streets of midtown Manhattan, one entered the Palladium by way of a grand, white marble staircase. Once inside, one encountered a huge circular dance floor, partially enclosed by a low railing, which was lined on the outside by backless couches, where people watched the dancing. Tables were on the left. On the ceiling, reams of elegant fabric gathered toward the center. And further contributing to the atmosphere was the fact that everyone *dressed* for an evening at the Palladium, donning suits, ties, wing-tip shoes, gold lamé, and sequins. According to Esmeralda Santiago, "The rest of the week, my mom was a seamstress in a sweatshop, and we were students in these really rough high schools; [but] the night you went to the Palladium, you were a princess."[43]

Claims such as Santiago's are consistently voiced with great detail and heart. The Palladium was a special place, where people shared space and moved in ways that were often impossible in the outside world. As Santiago explains, "These men were total strangers to me, and yet I could get on the dance floor with them and they could get me to do things I couldn't do on my own, in front of all these people, because we were both connected to the rhythm and what the rhythm meant."[44] Ernie Ensley, a famous dancer at the Palladium who also taped the nightly music, remembers, "They didn't care if you were black or white, as long as you could dance."[45] Max Salazar, a writer and radio host who frequented the Palladium, explains, "It was the dancers' home away from home, a weekend escape from the everyday problems of life."[46]

Still, despite these real sentiments of belonging and escape, the dance hall contained skewed power dynamics, even though it was remarkably integrated for its time. Piri Thomas, who painfully learned while growing up in East Harlem that "I'm black, and it don't make no difference whether I say good-by or adiós," complicates narratives of nighttime escape in his memoir, *Down These Mean Streets*.[47] In a passage resembling Santiago's claims about transforming into a princess, Thomas describes nightlife in Spanish Harlem:

> The lights transform everything into life and movement and blend the different colors into a magic cover-all that makes the drabness and garbage, wailing kids and tired people invisible. Shoes and clothes that by day look beat and worn out, at night take on a reflected splendor that the blazing multicolored lights burn on them. Everyone seems to develop a sense of urgent rhythm and you get the impression that you have to walk with a sense of timing. The daytime pain fades alongside the feeling of belonging.[48]

Thomas voices a sentiment not present in Santiago's claim. In this passage, his deep senses of daytime and nighttime exist alongside each other. The pleasure that comes with nighttime's urgent rhythms, and even the splendor he sees in people's clothing, becomes significant "alongside" a kind of pain that "fades" but does not entirely disappear. Even while registering their nighttime invisibility, Thomas's description of the "wailing kids and tired people" refuses to elide their presence.

At one point in Thomas's memoir, just a few pages after his observations about nighttime in Harlem, he makes his way to the Palladium. Rather than enter the ballroom as if stepping into a utopian space of nighttime royalty and glamour, Thomas quickly makes his way to the packed bathroom, where the sweet smell of pot mingles with the acrid smell of piss. Not wanting to risk shooting up in a public space, Thomas quickly snorts his heroin before heading out to the dance floor, where "the well-timed beat of hundreds of feet made a *chevere* noise on the wooden floor."[49] Clearly, the Palladium was not one space but many, where pleasure often existed alongside pain. Moreover, Thomas's decision to snort his heroin, made with a keen sense of surveillance, suggests that the world outside of the Palladium still permeated its walls.

This permeation affected how people arranged themselves, in relation both to the Palladium's architecture and to each other. As in any period in history, "appropriate" ways of moving in midcentury New York were strongly influenced by gender, sexuality, and race. Certain ways of moving received praise, while others produced a range of negative consequences, depending on who was moving, in what context. In her memoir, *When Spirits Dance Mambo: Growing Up Nuyorican in El Barrio,* Marta Vega frequently notes the difference in how her older brother, an avid Palladium dancer, and the girls in her family were taught to carry themselves and move through space. For example, while her brother, whose reputation as a "ladies' man" pleased their father greatly, was able to date multiple women and practice his dance routines with abandon, she and her elder sister, Chachita, were told to do nothing of the sort. Vega explains: "Increasingly often, Mami admonished my sister to keep her legs closed and not believe everything guys told her. . . . Annoyed, Chachita responded, 'My legs are nailed shut.'"[50] Although to "keep your legs shut" is a common expression, its vigorous repetition literally shaped behavior, affecting how the two sisters sat at school, on the stoop, or when meeting the parents of friends.

Such norms also affected how people moved within the Palladium. In general, women at the Palladium sat on couches, waiting to dance, while the men "cruised" around looking for their next partners. Men and women moved differently on the dance floor as well. Eddie Torres notes that certain shines are more popular among women, while others are more popular among men, partially corresponding to personal taste but also having to do with norms of social propriety. He explains: "Out of all the steps that I teach, I notice that the girls use a lot of the steps that I think are more appropriate and more flattering to them. So, it becomes like a menu, a choice for them to pick and choose which of these steps they're really going to use in a social setting. And there's a lot of these quick jumpy steps that the guys like and you may never see the girls doing that in a nightclub because it doesn't seem to flatter them or it's not to their taste."[51]

At the Palladium, the men tended to be flashier in their dancing than the women, with large moves and spread legs as opposed to small steps and swiveling hips. Nevertheless, contrary to the steps that Torres taught, the space of open shines at the Palladium offered dancers both a challenge and an opportunity to interact with social constraints in thrilling ways. When considering the options available and the consequences for moving one way rather than another in the Palladium, it becomes clear that dance conventions do not exist in static opposition to or in a separate sphere from the social conventions present in everyday life. In a space where no next move was ready and waiting, women occasionally burst through social expectations, filling their open shines with shimmying shoulders and spacious kicks. Dressed like a conservative schoolgirl in a full white skirt and starched collared shirt, one woman in *The Spirit Moves* not only shimmies her chest but repeatedly kicks her right leg forward and then arches back, egging her partner to do the same. She smiles as she flings her wide-open gestures, suggesting exhilaration in moving beyond gendered modes of normative public movement, if only briefly. Her flat shoes give her a sporty look, and before long, her male partner begins to swivel, also bending gendered expectations.

In addition to gender norms, wealth and racial difference also stratified patrons at the Palladium, creating additional tight places. Thompson notes that visitors entering the dance hall would have seen "amazing concentric circles of class and focus, an outer circle of rich visitors and celebrities seated at tables by the side of the dance floor, an inner circle of Latino and black dancing connoisseurs seated on the floor communally, and, in the sovereign center, the star dancers themselves. Such was the spatial logic of the Palladium during Wednesday night contests and performances."[52]

On Wednesday nights, the dancer Frank Piro, an East Harlem–born Italian American known as "Killer Joe" for his ability to outlast others on the dance floor, gave dance lessons from eight to nine P.M., before the Palladium's weekly mambo contest and performance began. Having honed his dancing skills at Harlem's Savoy Ballroom as a teenager, Piro served in the marines and won the "servicemen's division" of a jitterbug contest held at the 1942 Harvest Moon Ball. He was the first white man to win the national competition. During the early 1940s, he spent much of his time dancing with hostesses at the Stage Door Canteen, a club on 44th Street that catered to armed forces on leave. A few years after the war, Piro began teaching at the Palladium, receiving fifteen dollars per week to teach the dance hall's patrons how to mambo. An hour before the Wednesday-night showcase, Piro conducted mass mambo lessons, where he led hundreds of dancers through the form's basic steps. A sinewy man of five feet six inches, Piro taught dancers mambo's rudimentary patterns, which partners depart from and return to in their open shines. The emphasis was on partnered steps and the basics of *clave,* rather than on improvisation, which, as a mode of making dance rather than the dance itself, is harder to teach.

Piro was a tremendous hit among novices and the celebrity set, and he opened the dance floor to patrons who otherwise might have felt ill equipped to dance. Nevertheless, after noting that "the master of ceremony is significantly white," Mura Dehn remarks: "The authentic Mambo dancers— Cubans and Puerto Ricans—never recognized Killer Joe. They dismissed him with a smile of disdain. He had no rank amongst them."[53] Later, still talking about Piro's role at the Palladium, Dehn remarks: "The Afro American folk dancers are the most intolerant non-integrational group. They would never admit an outsider into their midst."[54] The point here is not that the Cuban and Puerto Rican dancers were the most "authentic." Millie Donay, an Italian American, was one of the most incredible mambo dancers in New York. Nor, by quoting Dehn, do I wish to suggest that African American dancers were less tolerant than other groups. Still, Dehn's observations challenge the abundant claims that race didn't matter at the Palladium.

Even the claims lauding the dance hall's integration reveal the racial tensions of the times. Describing how the Palladium shifted across various nights of the week, José Torres explains: "The audience was never exclusively Latin. A pattern soon established itself. On Wednesday nights when 'Killer Joe' Piro gave dance lessons, the crowd was Jewish and Italian. Friday was for Puerto Ricans, Saturday for Hispanics of all origins . . . and Sunday . . . was for American blacks. *Everybody* danced to Latin music."[55] It's significant that while Torres proudly emphasizes the fact that *"everybody"* danced to Latin music, his description suggests that, for the most part, they did so on different nights of the week.

Money also played a role in how bodies moved within the Palladium. One sees this in the remark that Morton agreed to the Sunday Latin matinee largely due to his "interest in green." The Palladium's interest in money drove its integration. On the flip side, though, people's ability to pay (or not) shaped the manner in which that integration occurred. According to Boggs, "Afro-Americans chose Sunday nights for several reasons; one main reason was cost: anyone coming before 10 P.M. paid only a dollar."[56] Moreover, while people generally talk about the Palladium as a place for leisure and entertainment, for many people, nights at the Palladium were a "job," no matter how satisfying. Consider, for example, the dancers hired by the Palladium to participate in its regular dance contests. Noting that people tended to clear the floor, sitting or gathering in circles to watch the Palladium's most stellar dancers, the Palladium soon instigated official amateur dance contests and elaborate mambo shows. Dance partners like Millie Donay and Pedro

Aguilar ("Cuban Pete"), and Ernie Ensley and Dotty Adams, became featured regulars.[57] Discussing the "amateur" dance teams, Ensley explains: "They had three dance teams—four dance teams—and they would put numbers on their backs and they would call them amateurs, right? . . . At that time, we were making fifteen dollars to dance in a contest; if we won it, we'd get five dollars more a piece—and would you believe we had to pay tax on that?"[58] According to Aguilar, the musicians, who received low wages at the Palladium, worked other jobs during the day, "in the garment district somewhere, or pushing carts, or as a busboy." At the pinnacle of mambo's popularity, "everything was at its height, except the paycheck."[59]

Numerous strictures existed within the Palladium, some consciously constructed, some not. As Ngugi wa Thiong'o explains, the space was not empty. Still, as evidenced by those who reminisce about the dance hall's integration and deep significance, there were exceptions to the Palladium's "spatial logic." Transgressions occurred on a nightly basis, seen in a particularly wide-open kick, or shimmying shoulders, a woman asking a man to dance, or even in a covert trip to the bathroom. As I will argue in the next section, these nightly interactions with a very full space achieved particular brilliance as dancers spun their open shines, choosing how to move in relation to mambo's formal strictures.

Clave 101: Improvising within the Form

The Palladium had a wide range of dancers, many of whom relied on crude imitation, or Joe Piro's classes, in order to get by. But the Palladium also had regular patrons who developed into eloquent improvisers through dedicated practice, learning mambo's rhythmic and choreographic structures in order to make choices within the form. By interacting with these formal constraints, each of them laden with cultural meaning, dancers creatively negotiated the social strictures that were at play not only in the Palladium but also in much of the outside world. The best improvisers typically occupied the southwest area of the ballroom, with circles of admirers gathering when dancers were really in a groove.[60] Thus Puerto Rican dancer Tommy Díaz's boast, "I cause circles."[61]

Eddie Torres, an acclaimed regular at the Palladium, explains that the Palladium's dancers, whom he calls the "first generation" of New York mamboists, were known for their exquisite open shines, which emphasized indi-

Figure 1. Pedro Aguilar and Millie Donay at the Palladium Ballroom, 1954. Photo by Yale Joel / Time Life Pictures / Getty Images.

vidual style. Recalling these "pioneers of open shines," Torres explains: "You saw literally like a dozen different styles and different ideas and people were into the idea of wanting to be themselves and express. They didn't want to look like you . . . and if they learned something from you they would try to twist it and turn it."[62] Still, Torres notes that these individual expressions always emerged in relation to complex structures: "There's laws and rules and regulations to almost everything that has to do with music and arts."[63] Similarly, when discussing the creativity of mambo's open shines, Dehn remarks: "Ballet and Africa, Spain and New York mix in an ecstatic marriage. It is an orgy of creativity. There is no question of right and wrong—there is only a question of satisfaction. I do not mean that there are no laws. It is the very appeal of these laws that provoke such passion."[64] As suggested by Dehn and Torres, dancers learned the rhythmic and choreographic patterns of mambo, which intersected with broader social strictures, and then used the improvisational space of open shines to interact creatively with these constraints.

At the Palladium, the *clave* was a particularly important structure to understand. Often considered the backbone of Afro-Caribbean music, the *clave* provided mambo's main organizing principle, within which both musicians and dancers improvised. According to "Cuban Pete":

> Everybody must take Clave 101 because it is like the foundation they put on the Empire State Building to build it, students need that foundation and knowledge in order to learn and apply steps to the dance. . . . The basics of Latin Dancing is that it goes to the five clicks of the *clave,* which fall within eight counts of music. . . . Dancing is about rhythm and the music tells you how to do it. Your ear is your third leg on the dance floor—without even knowing it.[65]

Despite its rigorous nature, this learning process was of course by no means restricted to classrooms. Cuban Pete's "Clave 101" began when a babysitter taught him to tap dance to a popular rumba called "El Manisero" (The Peanut Vender). This was how he began to feel rhythm. His mother also taught him dances like the *danzón* and the *guajira* for parties held at his aunts' houses. Eventually, he became friends with Raoul Batista, the nephew of Cuba's president Fulgencio Batista, and would visit Cuba often, avidly watching dance and listening to the rhythms of *guajuanco, yanyigo,* and *rumba. Finally, his* education came from musicians. Aguilar explains, "Yes, Machito, Bobby Escoto, José Borbuello, and Miguelito Valdéz helped me understand that you must not dance to the music, but inside the music."[66]

Because not everyone on the Palladium's dance floor received this education, deeply bound with cultural upbringing, the dance hall's Latin nights were both fraught and politically significant. In 1959, Piro exclaimed in the *New York Times:* "The general public in this country is square. . . . They don't understand Latin rhythm."[67] This claim is obviously problematic in that it excludes those who understand "Latin rhythm" from the "general public." Still, Piro's statement rightly suggests that rhythm constitutes a profound type of cultural knowledge. People become accustomed to particular rhythms not only in the art they consume and produce but also in the ebb and flow of everyday life. Rhythm is thus far more than a purely formal constraint.

Henri Lefebvre, a Marxist sociologist known for his writings on everyday life, understood this. Lefebvre began to analyze rhythm in the third volume of his *Critique of Everyday Life* (1981) and then coauthored two essays on the subject with his wife, Catherine Régulier: "The Rhythmanalytical Project" and "Attempt at the Rhythmanalysis of Mediterranean Cities." He continued to explore relations between rhythm and quotidian life (the repetitions that happen every day) in *Elements of Rhythmanalysis* (1992).[68] Of particular interest for our discussion of mambo, Lefebvre repeatedly emphasized the importance of the body in his rhythmanalytical project. For Lefebvre, bodies are ethically charged sites where multiple rhythms converge. He explains, "This human body is the site and place of interaction between the biological, the physiological (nature) and the social (often called the cultural) where each of these levels, each of these dimensions, has its own specificity, therefore its space-time: its rhythm."[69] Excepting a few strange moments when Lefebvre too quickly associates the corporeal with the natural, or rhythmic discord with illness, he (much like Foucault) usefully notes that bodies are socially produced—trained and disciplined to move *rhythmically* in particular ways, which differ across time and place. Interestingly, for Lefebvre, the analysis of rhythm requires an oscillation between outside observations and an awareness of one's lived, bodily experience. This is a dancer's work: "Externality is necessary; and yet in order to grasp a rhythm one must have been grasped by it, have given or abandoned oneself 'inwardly' to the time that is rhythmed. Is it not like this in music and in dance?"[70]

In their discussion of Latin/a dance, Delgado and Muñoz make observations similar to Lefebvre's. But they also make the political claim that rhythmic awareness and multiple conceptions of time enable the performance of "oppositional histories."[71] In making this argument, they refer to Gayatri Spivak's "Time and Timing: Law and History," where (like Lefebvre, who analyzes the force of repetition in capitalist production cycles upon lived circadian rhythms) Spivak distinguishes between "Time," a hegemonic chronological motion, and "Timing," the more fluid chronological motion of "life and ground level history."[72] Delgado and Muñoz equate *clave* with "timing," which has the potential to "sound over and through 'Time' as 'Law.'"[73] If one admits this link and then reconsiders Piro's claim, one begins to see the political stakes and cultural resistance involved in performing rhythms that the "general [hegemonic] public" doesn't understand.

Of particular importance for dance studies, Muñoz and Delgado further explain that Spivak's ground-level "Timing" must be analyzed as something embodied. They make this argument by way of Muniz Sodré, who states, "Rhythm as a way of structuring time is also a way of seeing and experiencing reality—it is constitutive of consciousness, not as an abstraction but as a physical force affecting all the organs of the body."[74] A keen example of this embodied sense of rhythm appears in Marta Vega's description of *clave,* where Vega urges the reader:

> Close your eyes and hold your breath. When the air feels like it's going to explode inside your chest, hold it longer. Now let it out. Listen. Listen to your heart and to the *ta-ta-ta-, ta-ta* of the *clave.* Let the clapping rhythm of those two mahogany sticks travel through your body, throbbing in every part of you. Know that if you do not move to the beat, you will burst. That's mambo.[75]

Rather than describe *clave* in abstract terms or compositional language, Vega describes it in terms of her body. She feels the rhythm in her chest and in her heart. This description comprises the opening paragraph of her memoir, her story of self.

Of course, this intimate knowledge of rhythmic constraint does not automatically correspond with identity. Not every black Cuban living in New York understands *clave* or views its implications in the same manner. Likewise, not everyone with white skin has a "square" sense of rhythm. One can *learn* rhythms. Katherine Dunham clearly recognizes this, for she emphasizes the training necessary to make skilled dancers. She explains: "This appreciation [of rhythm] is not based on any physical difference, nor is it psychological; we are sociologically conditioned by our constant contact with it, and it continues from babyhood up. . . . But that does not mean there is no technique. There is."[76]

The challenge then is to become intimately familiar with rhythmic structures, in this case the *clave,* without losing one's ability to make spontaneous choices. This is no easy task. Eddie Torres, who spent his teenage years dancing at the Palladium, learning his skills informally on the dance floor, has formalized mambo technique in recent decades by studying musical time signatures and naming the steps that he developed over the years through open shines. According to Torres, this formal education has taken a toll on his ability to improvise. He explains, "It's a beautiful thing to have education, but . . . I think you also [lose] a certain spontaneity."[77] Torres illustrates this loss by comparing his dancing to that of a Cuban friend from childhood, Roberto.[78] Torres claims that, if they were to dance side-by-side, Roberto would grab people's attention every time. Whereas his own dancing now has a "structured look to it," Torres explains that Roberto's open shines are full of round moves and poetry, flowing from one movement to the next, even if he doesn't know, for example, whether he breaks on the two or the three.

Torres explains that Roberto doesn't want to study with him or join his professional company because he fears that an "education" would hamper his ability to improvise:

> He says, "You [Torres] took the dance out of the jungle and you brought it into the studio, civilized it with the timing, structure, and the theory, but you paid a big price for it. . . . I watch you dance now, and now you are the civilized Eddie Torres, who takes steps by names and by beats and structures them together, all beautiful, but you've lost that eye of the tiger, that animal instinct that used to be the Eddie Torres in the night club, where you would not even open your eyes and you would be in such a trance of dance and nothing had any structure to it. You just looked like a wildcat out in the jungle just being natural in your habitat."[79]

Although both Roberto and Torres are phenomenal mamboists whom one must take seriously, their conversation is troubling, at least at first glance. One of this book's primary goals is to challenge simple claims that reduce improvisational skill to "animal instinct," whose natural habitat is the "jungle." All too often, the link between improvisation and animality (a common trope, bound with reductive ideas about instinct) has pejorative and often racist undertones.[80] Akira Lippit's *Electric Animal: Toward a Rhetoric of Wildlife* (2000) and Giorgio Agamben's *The Open: Man and Animal* (2002), both of which analyze the defining role of animality in Western philosophy, provide intellectual and historical context for the link between animality and improvisation. Both authors note that in the history of Western philosophy, man repeatedly has defined his nature in opposition to the animal, a critical move that elevates rationality over instinct. Once one recognizes the binary between man and animal as a false construction, alternatives emerge to the merely pejorative understanding of "animalistic dancing."

Still, it is still necessary to acknowledge the importance of education in Roberto's dancing. It's problematic that neither Roberto nor Torres sees his early dancing as a form of training—and that Torres seems to experience it as a constraint or inhibiting factor in his improvising. This notion reflects a dominant cultural hierarchy that associates freedom with a certain kind of knowledge and then regrets the other kinds of knowledge that it seemed to displace. Although Roberto suggests otherwise, Roberto's dancing *does* require technique and a very keen sense of rhythm, even if he can't describe it in counted measures. Dancers often acquire this understanding in kitchens, or on the street, or on a variety of dance floors, but this too constitutes an "education." As Dunham explains, there *is* technique involved. Furthermore, although Torres claims to have lost a degree of spontaneity in his dancing, a formalist "education" does not necessarily dampen one's ability to improvise. In fact, in many cases, it improves one's improvisational eloquence. Cuban Pete, who believed everyone should take "Clave 101," was phenomenal on the dance floor, exacting quick rhythmic turns and extending his long legs in front of his body, halting on a dime before reentering the music's pulse. Similarly, the drummer Tito Puente, one of Torres's most significant teachers, clearly knew music theory, and yet he was a brilliant improviser.

Circle-gathering improvisations at the Palladium were not a temporal free-for-all, but rather an ongoing series of negotiations with rhythmic structures, whether they were consciously learned or absorbed in a more intuitive manner. In order to make improvised choices (which is not to imply a rigid opposition between instinct and rationality), one must develop a sense of how one's own body pulses—how it moves habitually and how it might move otherwise—in relation to its surrounding rhythms, which are neither static nor essential. If a rhythmic structure sounds deeply within one's body, then one can improvise exquisitely in relation to it, whether that means dragging behind the beat, anticipating its punctuation, or accentuating the break. This is where the political power of improvisation exists most strongly. Otherwise, no matter how smooth or "eye-catching" one's movements are, one is really just moving around.

In addition to *clave,* dancers at the Palladium made spontaneous choices about shape and sequencing. Interestingly, just as Piro witnessed a clash of rhythms on the dance floor, the *New York Times* dance critic John Martin witnessed a clash of postures, also resulting from diverse training and cultural knowledge. As with rhythm, mambo's choreographic principles were socially far more complicated than "formalist" structures seem to suggest. Making a clear connection between expressive culture and Roosevelt's 1933 inaugural address, Martin claims:

> Unhappily for the good-neighbor policy, it is the South American dances that look oddest; and that is perfectly natural, for there are subtleties in the movements of other peoples that are hard to acquire. The basic difficulty in these particular dances is one of posture; the Ibero-Americans center their bodies differently from their Northern neighbors, and until

that difference has been conquered no North American can expect to do the Caribbean and South American dances with conviction.[81]

Martin then declares that although the "white man" has great difficulty doing these unfamiliar dances, "there is no reason why he should not try . . . if he does not care how he looks (and he doesn't!), for the dances are truly wonderful and the music superb."[82]

Martin simply declares what is "odd" and what is "fine," suggesting that the imitation or appropriation of expressive forms has no consequence beyond entertainment. Given the context, it is difficult not to cringe at the phrase "until that difference has been conquered." Moreover, in referring to "racial posture," Martin implies a racial understanding of bodily comportment rather than recognizing the importance of tradition, discipline, and cultural mores in shaping the body's stance. Still, Martin's observations suggest something worth thinking about: that it is challenging to dance in unfamiliar styles, but that it can be socially meaningful to do so. Dancers and pedestrians alike learn distinct ways of moving in different spheres of life, which demands the acquisition of multiple techniques. It is difficult to break habitual patterns of movement, and techniques frequently interfere with each other, even within a single body. Whether or not the dancers witnessed by John Martin were aware of technique's hold, his lighthearted yet disparaging remarks reference the outward signs of a clash of techniques.

Far from the aesthetic failings suggested by Martin, these glitches call attention to society's constructed notions of beauty and the status quo and signal attempts to step outside of habitual, comfortable ways of moving. These glitches disappear with choreography, as dancers rehearse set sequences for hours, trying to diminish any signs of struggle or mental effort. But with improvised social dancing at places like the Palladium, these "glitches" signal unique and unpredictable encounters with a constantly shifting scene. Rather than looking on voyeuristically, as an anthropologist might, or employing strategies of avoidance, people on the Palladium's dance floor tried to dance with each other, constantly negotiating the social norms, distinct cultural histories, and diverse physical techniques that become pronounced in a room full of difference.

When discussing the early years of mambo's development in New York, Torres claims that mambo became an open repository of forms, enriched by the cultural diversity present in places like the Palladium. He explains:

> The beauty of the development [of mambo] in New York was that in the halls . . . where it was multinational, you would have people of all ethnic backgrounds. You had input from all these different nationalities. You know, you had the Anglo-Americans from the ballroom world putting in their beautiful ideas of arm styling and attitude, and then you had of course the blacks from New York City with their nice funky really hoe-down type attitude. They were bringing that into the mambo. So, the mambo became a dance of all nationalities, where everyone had an input on it and the development was eclectic. . . . So, this is why I think it appealed to all because people were able to say, "I can put my ballroom and I can put my African movement in here, and I can put my Peabody."[83]

This sense of belonging has deep significance, and a wide stylistic range certainly appears in recordings of mambo from the early 1950s. But, as I've argued throughout this chapter, Torres's account is too simple. In a public dance hall like the Palladium, egalitarian power relations are not automatic, and there is no guarantee that contact will yield positive outcomes. The various encounters that took place on a moment-to-moment basis were fraught and extremely live. However, it is precisely in relation to this complex, shifting scene that the possibility for meaningful exchange emerges, as does the vital, political power of improvisation.

Night after night, dancers moved their own bodies in relation to a floor full of difference, responsible for their own production, even as they were influenced by the moves of others. This responsibility increased the dancers' chance of being transformed by the experience, as were many of the dancers who frequented the Palladium: Pedro Aguilar, Millie Donay, Ernie Ensley, and Esmeralda Santiago. It is in mambo's improvised breaks that dancers at the Palladium sought ways to sound out deeply embedded oppositional histories, dancing subaltern Timings against Time. It is also in these improvised breaks that dancers sought ways to engage with difference and to make something creative out of disorientation. Undoubtedly, there must have been failures, or instances where social constraints were too tight for improvisational exuberance. It is nevertheless in these improvised breaks—understood as live, urgent, playful, intelligent, spontaneous interactions with constraint—in short, as *practices* of freedom—that mambo's open shines begin to deserve their name.

CHAPTER 2 *We Insist! Seeing Music and Hearing Dance*

Salón México (1948), a film about a showgirl at one of Mexico's famous cabarets, contains striking scenes of mambo in which distinctions between musicians and dancers begin to blur. While musicians in the film typically begin to play from set locations—either on a bandstand or outside a circle of observers—they head to the dance floor, mingling and moving in time with the dancers. In one extraordinary scene, a trumpeter, playing a Havana-style *danzón*-mambo, breaks to the floor and rolls slowly toward the camera, moving languidly in time with the music. Another musician urges him on from behind, swiveling his hips and stepping in syncopated time while sounding a rich *clave* on two wooden sticks. The trumpeter rolls all the way across the stage, leaning his head over its edge, prone and near falling as he blows through his horn. The camera zooms in on the trumpet's circular, brassy mouth, with the musician's horizontal body forming a hazy dancing background.[1]

This blurring of roles was not merely a cinematic fiction. Across midcentury dance halls, a variety of social dances developed alongside vibrant traditions of improvised music, with musicians and dancers depending upon each other for inspiration. As noted earlier, Tito Puente, Tito Rodríguez, and Machito battled for the hearts of dancers at the Palladium. Similarly, the dancer Leon James recalls the back-and-forth interaction between Dizzy Gillespie and dancers: "Every time [Gillespie] played a crazy lick, we cut a crazy step to go with it. And he dug us and blew even crazier stuff to see if we could dance to it, a kind of game, with the musicians and dancers challenging each other."[2] Perhaps most interesting, as seen in *Salón México,* many musicians actually danced while playing, both in dance halls and in more austere musical settings. Thelonious Monk is a well-known example of a pianist who would start dancing when the music was really "happening." According to the drummer Ben Riley, "if the music wasn't going the way Monk really wanted it, then he wouldn't dance."[3] Riley describes his relationship with Monk as being like playing drums with a tap dancer: "You see, the tap dancer would set up a certain rhythm, and then you'd have a chance to either correspond or play that rhythm again. And to me, that's the kind of situation that I had with Thelonious, it's like we were dancing with each other."[4]

Despite these deep relationships, in the West, dance and music are analyzed consistently as distinct entities: one historically female, the other historically male; one of the body, the other of the mind; one seen, the other heard. Gavin Bryars, who founded the Portsmouth Sinfonia and the Music Department at Leicester Polytechnic, is a rare musician who recognizes the corporeality of music, especially when it is improvised. However, he rejected improvisation midway through his career for precisely that reason. Bryars states that in 1975, after years spent working as a bassist, he abandoned improvisation due to its inevitable corporeality. He explains: "One of the main reasons I am against improvisation now is that in any improvising position the person creating the music is identified with the music. . . . It's like standing a painter next to his picture so that every time you see the painting you see the painter as well and you can't see it without him. And because of that the music, in improvisation, doesn't stand alone. It's corporeal."[5]

Although Bryars smartly observes that audience members have a hard time separating improvising musicians from their music, he strangely equates corporeality entirely with a *seen* body. But this is too simple. A rigorous discussion of improvisation's corporeality demands that one recognize the materiality, sensual complexity, and historical weight that exists within, and presses upon, bodies. Such complex corporeality can be seen with particular clarity in improvisational collaborations between musicians and dancers, not only in popular dance halls such as the Palladium but also in avant-garde performance contexts typically construed as being part of a "high" art tradition. It is important to analyze relations between both spheres of performance and to consider why such relations are so often elided in performance histories and critical studies of improvisation. Dianne McIntyre studied with dancers from New York's Savoy Ballroom—a block-long dance hall in Harlem—and strove to integrate dance hall techniques such as improvisational breaks with her modern dance training. What's more, she felt it would be culturally dishonest not to do so.

Moving from the Palladium Ballroom, but continuing to think about relations between music and dance, this chapter discusses the improvisational work of Judith Dunn and Bill Dixon and of Dianne McIntyre's company, Sounds in Motion. All three artists worked to create ensembles where neither music nor dance was subordinate to the other. Improvising together, musicians identified as dancers and dancers identified as musicians. These radical collaborations challenged typical divisions between "high" and "low" forms of expression, the relation between gendered traditions of postmodern improvised dance and jazz, and the assumed whiteness of the "avant-garde." Presenting audiences with a body that is both seen and heard, they also demanded a sensually complex mode of reception from their audience. Vision alone could not grasp the politics of the ensemble's improvisational work.

Perhaps most important for the book's larger discussion of relations between improvisation and freedom, the collaborations in this chapter reveal artists working through notions of freedom that were oftentimes in conflict with one another. Examples abound: Judith Dunn found chance procedures to be a liberating way to make dances early in her career, while Bill Dixon found the compositional choices available in such a method to be limiting; Dunn was terrified by the notion of improvising in performance, while Dixon felt uncomfortable when asked to move like a dancer while playing; Abbey Lincoln found new possibilities under the umbrella of "jazz," while many musicians found the label to be reductive and at times demeaning. Although I focus on a few performances in this chapter, namely McIntyre's collaboration with Max Roach and Abbey Lincoln in a 1980 performance of *The Freedom Now Suite,* I am most interested in the improvisational *practices* that these dancers and musicians developed in relation to various kinds of constraint. While it may seem that these artists differed from those in the previous chapter insofar as they worked within a concert tradition rather than a dance hall, I hope to illustrate that their formal choices were never separate from the broader social world in which they lived and worked.

Judith Dunn and Bill Dixon: A Galvanizing Duo

Judith Dunn's dance career did not begin until after she graduated from Brooklyn College with a major in anthropology, even though she came from a dance background insofar as her mother studied with Martha Graham before eventually becoming a physical therapist. In 1955, Dunn abandoned her plans to attend graduate school in anthropology in order to enter the dance program at Sarah Lawrence, where she received her master's degree. Soon afterward, she began teaching dance at Brandeis University. Dunn was an enthusiastic and committed instructor, whose work with students pushed her own choreography. She recalls: "I was afraid I didn't know anything. Sometimes I think I must be the only dancer who learned how to dance by teaching dancing."[6] During this time, Dunn captured the attention of Merce Cunningham, who taught a few classes while passing through Boston. Inspired by Cunningham's encouragement, Dunn began to work with new vigor and in 1958 joined the Merce Cunningham Dance Company, where she remained for five years.

While many postmodern choreographers were influenced by jazz principles of improvisation, choreographers such as Merce Cunningham, along with John Cage, Cunningham's longtime partner and musical collaborator, also took a tremendous interest in Chinese, Japanese, and Indian philosophies that emphasized the physical properties of objects and cultivated an awareness of the concentration necessary to engage fully in unanticipated acts. Cunningham and Cage were particularly interested in Zen philosophy, as put forth by Daisetz Suzuki. According to Susan Foster, "Both artists used Zen as inspiration to concentrate attention on the physical and sonic facts of performance. Rather than implement dance movement and musical sound to convey an underlying message or transcendental property such as beauty, they opened up their respective mediums to a newly concrete participation in art-making and viewing."[7] While improvisation was never a deep part of the collaborations between Cunningham and Cage, where performers had few choices in determining how performances would unfold, the two did use chance procedures to develop material. Cunningham would flip coins or roll dice to determine where and when dancers would enter and exit the stage or to designate the length of phrases. Dancers often had no idea what sound score would accompany them until they appeared on stage. Cunningham and Cage borrowed these strategies from the Taoist I Ching, believing that chance allowed them to distance the creative process from the artist's intentions.

These procedures strongly influenced Judith Dunn. From 1960 to 1962, many of Cunningham's dancers, along with a handful of musicians and visual artists, participated in a choreography workshop taught by Dunn's husband, Robert Ellis Dunn, at Cunningham's studio in the Living Theater building, located on 14th Street and 6th Avenue. Robert Dunn played piano for dance classes across New York City. He also studied music theory with John Cage at the New School for Social Research, and this informed both his attitude toward composition and his teaching style. Having witnessed composition classes taught by the highly dramatic choreographer Doris Humphrey and the obsessed-with-structure composer Louis Horst, Dunn tried to lead a less rigid class. His students had leeway in how they chose to fulfill assignments, and they spent a great deal of time talking about their work. Heavily influenced by Cage, Dunn exposed his students to the indeterminate structures of composers such as Pierre Boulez and Karleheinz Stockhausen.

In addition to providing ways to think about indeterminacy and new time structures, these composers introduced new ways of notating music, employing them not merely to create fixed scores that allowed new sounds but also as a way to write down flexible parameters for a work that performers could then interpret in various ways. These scoring methods were important in Robert Dunn's composition class, enabling dancers to objectify and better talk about their work and their processes. According to Dunn, "[Rudolph von] Laban's idea was very secondarily to make a *Tanzschrift,* a dance-writing, a way to record. Laban's idea was to make a *Schriftanz,* to use graphic—written—inscriptions and then to generate activities. Graphic notation is a way of inventing the dance. It is part of the conception of the dance."[8]

So, while the students in Dunn's composition class became keenly interested in the physical properties of quotidian movement—not just modernist dance "vocabulary"—and began to incorporate chance and improvisation into their work, they were also taught to be writers with elaborate, but open, scores. Trisha Brown, who studied in Robert Dunn's workshops and went on to perform with the Judson Dance Theater, explains that the rigor of structured improvisation differs from a self-indulgent dance of whimsy, which she calls "therapy or catharsis or your happy hour."[9] She states:

> If in the beginning you set a structure and decide to deal with X, Y, and Z materials in a certain way, nail it down even further and say you can only walk forward, you cannot use your voice or you have to do 195 gestures before you hit the wall at the other end of the room, that is an improvisation within set boundaries. That is the principle, for example, behind jazz. The musicians may improvise, but they have a limitation in the structure just as improvisation in dance does.[10]

As seen in Brown's desire to distance improvised dance from mere "therapy or catharsis or your happy hour," structured limitations appealed to dancers, lending improvised dance a formal rigor and seriousness that was thought to be lacking by early modernists who kept improvisation off the concert stage as they struggled for "high" art legitimacy.

Five students attended Dunn's first workshop in the fall of 1960: Paulus Berenson, Marni Mahaffay, Simone (Forti) Morris, Steve Paxton, and Yvonne Rainer. In the next session, Ruth Allphon joined along with Judith Dunn, who was still performing with Cunningham's company. By the fall of 1961, Brown, Deborah Hay, Alex Hay, and Elaine Summers were some of the new students, with occasional visits by Remy Charlip, Robert Morris, Jill Johnston, and Robert Rauschenberg.[11] Although seldom noted in history books, Judith Dunn quickly assumed an important teaching role, with people referring to the workshop as the Dunns' class. According to Elaine Summers, "My feeling is that Judith was teaching alongside of Robert. I remember Robert sitting at the piano and Judith beside the piano, Robert giving out the assignment and Judith participating in it. The extraordinary thing about the class was the clarity of the presentation of Cage's principles, and the clarity of the teaching structure, which both Robert and Judith participated in."[12]

This group of creative individuals soon branched out from the contained workshop environment, publicly presenting its first evening of work in the summer of 1962. Performing regularly between1962 and 1964 at Judson Memorial Church, at 55 Washington Square South in the West Village, the group assumed the name Judson Dance Theater. While much of the work presented at Judson valued spontaneity, one of the group's final performances consisted almost entirely of structured improvisations. Concert #14, presented on April 27, 1964, consisted of two parts. The first half of the evening contained seven improvisations that were "choreographed" by Carla Blank and Sally Gross, Lucinda Childs, Judith Dunn, Alex Hay and Robert Rauschenberg, Steve Paxton, and Yvonne Rainer. These seven scored improvisations could occur in any order, at any time. During intermission, the audience changed places, and then Deborah Hay presented a twenty-five-minute improvisation.[13]

Reflecting on the demise of the Judson Dance Theater, Jill Johnston, the dance and art critic for the *Village Voice* from 1959 to 1968, pays particular attention to this improvised concert, noting that it fell flat despite its "minimal restrictions on freedom" and its impressive collection of vanguard dancers. She argues that the performers were too polite and that no "necessity" emerged out of the "collective atmosphere of private sideshows."[14] Here, Johnston's dissatisfaction resembles a significant critique of Judson Church and highlights the self-indulgence within Judson's explorations. Perhaps more important, especially when considering the relation between these postmodern experiments in improvised dance and jazz, Johnston notes a conflict between the evening's supposed freedom and its private self-absorption. While the Judson Dance Theater operated as a collective, the individuals who worked under its auspices had their own insular curiosities. Around the time of Concert #14's improvisations, the clarity of Judson's interests began to dissipate, and the dancers broke away to embark on their own pursuits. As Summers recounts, "Judson was a complex, bubbling, boiling, hot place, full of people really working on their ideas and getting their ideas out, and being involved in the opportunity to 'do their own thing,' with a commitment not to get in each other's way."[15] But, in the end, this experiment was too difficult to sustain.

Like many of the Judson artists, such as Paxton, Rainer, and Brown, Judith Dunn would continue to hone her craft and question assumptions within the field, particularly through her collaborations with the trumpeter Bill Dixon. It soon became clear that freedom from the conventions of modern dance did not necessarily entail freedom in a broader social sense, particularly if that freedom was construed as some sort of destination or arrival. The two artists met in November 1965, when Dunn heard Dixon play in *Black Zero,* a multimedia performance organized by Aldo Tambellini at the Astor Playhouse in New York City. Tambellini, a pioneer in the video art movement during the late 1960s, had invited Dixon and the bassist Alan Silva to play as part of a turbulent performance that included the work of Benn Morea, Ron Hahne, Elsa Tambellini, and Calvin Herton, in conjunction with the inflation of a giant weather balloon and projections of film strips that Tambellini had painted and chemically treated.[16] According to Dixon (echoing Gavin Bryars's observations about the hypervisibility of improvised music), he hadn't reached the point in his career where he wanted to be seen while playing, unless on a proscenium stage, because he thought it would be distracting. Yet there he was, highly visible, playing with Alan Silva in an intimate cinemateque.[17]

Short on cash, Dixon had a five-dollar-a-month answering service. The day after the Tambellini performance, he received a phone call from Judith Dunn. Having seen the show, Dunn asked Dixon to come to the New Dance Group to see a dance piece she was making. Soon afterward, Dunn and

Dixon embarked on a collaboration that lasted the next eight years. In addition to creating striking improvised works, their collaborations explored and openly acknowledged relations between black traditions of improvised music and the rather white world of postmodern dance.

Born on Nantucket Island in 1925, Dixon grew up in Harlem. From an early age, he began studying visual art at a Works Progress Administration school in Manhattan. After returning from an army tour during World War II, Dixon studied music at Manhattan's Harnette School. At the time of his meeting with Dunn, Dixon was involved heavily in a black music scene, having organized and produced the October Revolution in Jazz in 1964, with performances and panel discussions by Cecil Taylor, Sun Ra, and Steve Lacy.[18] During this time, a black vanguard emerged that preferred to think of its music as "black music," or "the music," rather than accept the label of "jazz," a category regarded as limiting and often pejorative. During the mid-1960s, Dixon worked amid an activist crowd, including the poet Amiri Baraka, the pianist Cecil Taylor, and the saxophonists Archie Shepp and John Coltrane. As with any movement, there was a range of positions, and Dixon shifted his views on black music throughout his career. In a 1967 article, "To Whom It May Concern," Dixon pondered: "Is the music black? . . . I don't know if one can accurately say music is black, white, green or indifferent. It's quite obvious, (if I'm seen) if I play, since I'm black and if I'm being honest, that I'm playing out of a so-called black experience. But then again, I'd prefer someone to say that I'm playing out of my own experience."[19]

Here, Dixon expresses ambivalence regarding the blackness of the music he plays while also highlighting the visual pathology of racism—the fact that his music becomes something different when he is seen. During the mid-1960s, Dixon was keenly aware of the limitations placed on black musicians: "Being a Black man in America can put incredible blinders on your vision. If I'm turned down for something, I don't know really whether it's because of the quality of my work or because I'm Black. That's been the history."[20] Of course, the Judson Dance Theater was also part of this history. Reflecting on the early years of his collaboration with Dunn, Dixon notes that he was never treated rudely by the postmodern dance scene in New York. Still, he recalls the existence of a subliminal racism and notes: "Something wasn't right. . . . Judson Church was a long five miles away from the work I was doing up at 91st street."[21]

Without doubt, the two artists had distinct artistic and cultural homes in

New York City. But through their research, performances, and teaching endeavors, they grappled with the differences between them. Throughout the mid-1960s, Dunn and Dixon performed in many venues for experimental dance, including the Judson Memorial Church and Dance Theater Workshop. By the late summer of 1967, they began to incorporate other dancers and musicians into their work and laid the foundations for the Bill Dixon–Judith Dunn [or vice versa] Company of Musicians and Dancers. They also taught extensively. During April 1967, they offered classes twice a week at Dunn's 6th Avenue loft. As with most of their classes, they were open to both musicians and dancers, offering a rare opportunity for artists working in different mediums not only to perform together but also to train and learn together. According to Dixon, "I would rehearse the musicians in one corner while Judy was working something out with the dancers in another corner; after an hour we would put it together, see how it would work, and mark off solos."[22] That same year, they also taught at DTW, the New Dance Group Studio, and Columbia University Teachers College.

In the fall of 1968, Dunn and Dixon began teaching part-time in the Dance Department at Bennington College, while Dixon also taught courses in black music aesthetics and history at the University of Wisconsin, Madison. The Bennington Dance Department was eager to have Dunn on board, but Dunn refused to accept their teaching invitation without Dixon. From the beginning, Dixon's presence in technique classes differed significantly from that of a customary accompanist.[23] Dixon recalls:

> Right away, I disagreed with the way dance classes were conducted. The dancers had to spend the first half hour as a warm-up, and I wondered, "Why don't they just come into the room warmed up?" The dancers were very unknowledgeable musically: they would take a piece of Webern, take a piece of George Russell, a little Schubert here at the beginning. . . . I was shocked. "Don't you people know what you are doing?" I stopped that immediately when I came to Bennington. Even the term, "music for dance" was offensive; music is for music. I had a great time, but I had to bring them around to my way of thinking. "NO, I don't play blues. NO, I don't do gospel. I don't do Chopin. I don't read fast enough to sit up there like an accompanist and go through something." I hit that room playing piano, and about a half hour after I started playing I looked up, and about fifty people were crowded into the room wondering what was going on. Judy had to say, "Now, this is Bill Dixon. He is not an accompanist, he's a musician-composer."[24]

JUDITH DUNN and BILL DIXON

Radcliffe Gym

THURSDAY MARCH 14

3-6:00 PM.

$1.50

For information
call:

UN4-8100
EXT. 3653

ORIGINAL EXERCISES FOLLOWED
BY GENERAL DISCUSSION TO SET THE PROBLEMS
FOR GROUP IMPROVISATIONS

experimental
dance composition class

"Miss Dunn and Dixon seek to create situations in which dance and music can exist together, can inhabit the same time and space, yet with neither subordinate to the other."

".... she may ask students to do unconventional, seemingly off-balance movements or familiar movements in a radically different pattern, such assignments kinesthetically "shaking up" the dancers until they are forced to observe and analyze their own way of moving."

".......to have the sound of a trumpet virtually get under your skin and into your being. The breath that makes the music becomes your breath as you move, driving you on to new, sharp reactions."

- from article by Jack Anderson, Dance Magazine, November 1967

MISS DUNN WAS FORMERLY A MEMBER OF THE MERCE CUNNINGHAM DANCE COMPANY. SHE IS BOTH A FOUNDING MEMBER OF AND A LEADING FIGURE IN THE JUDSON DANCE THEATER, JUDSON MEMORIAL CHURCH, NEW YORK.

Figure 2. Flyer for experimental dance class, 1968.

Although Dixon became affiliated with Bennington through the Dance Department, in the spring of 1974, describing blackness not as a color but rather as an "attitude," he founded the Black Music Division, where he remained on faculty until 1996.[25] Even in a liberal college environment, tensions were high. Dixon recalls that when he arrived at Bennington in 1968, "there wasn't a black pair of shoes on the campus."[26]

A core group of students at Bennington quickly became enthralled by Dunn and Dixon's teaching methods, their charisma, and their work—all of which had political implications. At the time, Bennington's dance faculty included Jane Dudley, Martha Whitman, Jack Moore, and Bill Bales, with Viola Farber there briefly as a visiting instructor. Most of Bennington's dance students (many of whom were highly trained) were versed in the modern traditions of Martha Graham, José Limón, and Merce Cunningham. Those who were intrigued by Dunn and Dixon immediately sensed that the artistic duo was doing something radical: they were an interracial couple (both professionally and romantically) teaching classes to musicians and dancers simultaneously where each form was given value. Moreover, they worked improvisationally and strove for rigor. Reflecting on this aspect of their work, Susan Sgorbati, a former student and current professor in the Bennington Dance Department, recalls that Dunn and Dixon treated improvisation with great intensity and utter seriousness, something that wasn't being done elsewhere in the realm of U.S. concert dance.[27] According to Sgorbati:

> When Judy came up to Bennington with Bill Dixon, the thing that they were experimenting with at the time was the performance of improvisation. That was a pretty radical idea at that point. Not that improvisation in itself was such a radical idea because that was always a part of dancing. But the idea that you would take it seriously as a form for performance was something very radical—that there might be skills involved, that it could be practiced, and that musicians and dancers were working as equals, meaning that music was not an accompaniment to the dance, and dancing wasn't just an explanation of the music. The idea that they were both running parallel and interacting was a key element to their work.[28]

According to Penny Campbell (a student at Bennington from 1966 to 1970, as well as an eventual teaching assistant and company member), "They would pose radical questions. People felt they were the fresh New York thing."[29] Campbell explains that Dixon's music was powerful and progres-

sive. "It changes lives," she said. Reminiscing further, Campbell notes that although she understood very little of what Dunn and Dixon were doing at the
time, she tried to look like Judy: "She was magical. Galvanizing."[30]

Throughout her career, Dunn challenged conventions within the realm of
New York concert dance, displaying a rebelliousness that carried over into
her teaching methodology. In Jack Anderson's "Judith Dunn and the Endless
Quest," Dunn discusses her frustration with the rules of most dance classes—
that dancers in technique classes move through long sequences in diagonal
lines and that compositional forms like ABA are taught as dogma, necessary
for the making of sound choreography. She found such rules stultifying.
Dunn also notes norms regarding style and physical comportment that re-
strict the dance world. Rebelling against the romantic look of ballet dancers,
Dunn immediately cut her hair upon joining the Cunningham Company.[31]
These choices also extended into formal concerns. For example, breaking
with spatial expectations, Dunn staged one of her first works in the round,
performing incredibly close to her audience. Like many of her Judson con-
temporaries, she also employed chance procedures and created intricate
scores for her dances in her early work. Explaining her initial use of graphs
and charts, Dunn states: "What made it so exciting was that our main concern was, ultimately, not methodology at all, despite the dice and the charts.
The methods we used for making dances were not ends, but means. Our real
purpose was a desire to abandon old habits and find new ways of moving.
The dice and the charts helped force us out of habit."[32]

Although Dunn learned a lot during the Judson years, she is quick to
highlight not only differences among individuals making work under the auspices of the Judson Dance Theater but also differences between her Judson
choreography and her later work with Dixon. Dunn's collaboration with
Dixon changed her choreographic procedures, challenging her to abandon
charts and to engage more fully in the rigor of improvisation. In the early
days of Dunn's work with Dixon, she was fascinated by improvisation but
found it difficult. She explains: "I had to come to terms with all of my defini-
tions of order and structure. I had to expand my ideas of what dance movement was and could be."[33] Dunn was accustomed to notating her dances, as-
siduously planning movement in advance, which she then performed in an
improvisational style. She was attentive to each moment, and like many Judson dancers, she tried to suggest the purity of doing movements for the first
time. But despite this "in the moment" quality, the work was mapped out be-

Figure 3. Flyer for performance by Judith Dunn and Bill Dixon at Judson Memorial Church, 1966.

forehand or subsumed by designed chance procedures. Dunn found this practice hard to abandon.

Dixon, however, was schooled within a tradition where musicians did not notate and then learn what to perform in an "improvisational style," but rather developed technique to better realize musical desires as they arose. For Dixon, training as an improviser constitutes an insistent kind of preparation—readying oneself to immediately seize musical ideas. Moreover, Dixon discusses technique as being pluralistic, rather than being a monolithic style handed down from the past. To better make one's own improvised choices, one must understand musical traditions and choices that other musicians have made. This approach clearly extends beyond the "private sideshows" noted by Jill Johnston when observing the improvisations of Judson Dance Theater. Reflecting on the chance procedures employed by the likes of Cage and Cunningham, and the Judson dancers who followed their lead, Dixon recalls:

> The funny thing about chance was—I never saw those people *taking* a chance. Now, Jazz players take a chance. I always disagreed with the philosophy of chance operations; I understand a bit more about it now, but it just doesn't work for me, because whatever [the chance offered you], you had to have the ability—intellectually, physically, and creatively—to carry the thing out. A lot of them would let the instructions do everything, so they never really *created* anything. When Judy and I worked with the music, I never used any of that, and eventually she stopped relying on it. I used to ask Judy in practice: "Why do you give yourself a barre? You're not going to do any of that. Why use it in practice if that's not what you're going to perform with?" . . . She began to see what the possibilities were, and by the time we started working together at Bennington, she was already into it.[34]

Heavily influenced by Dixon's approach to improvisation, Dunn abandoned charts and graphs and the "control" that they seemed to offer. She improvised an entire evening's performance for the first time in the summer of 1966 at the Newport Jazz Festival, where Dunn and Dixon presented *Pomegranate,* a thirty-seven-minute work in collaboration with Ken McIntyre (bass clarinet), Louis Brown (tenor saxophone), Bob Cunningham (double bass), and Tom Price (percussion).[35] With the performance set in the round, Dunn had most of the stage in which to dance, choosing to lie on the floor when she wasn't performing, resembling the relaxed postures that musicians assume when others in the ensemble take their solos. As with most of Dunn and Dixon's work at the time, few people reviewed the Newport performance. When asked why their collaboration is largely absent from history books as well as archival sources, Dixon notes, "The history that gets written is the history that's permissible."[36] In any case, neither dance nor music critics gave them much attention. Of those in the music world who did (Elisabeth van der Mei, Dan Morgenstern, and Whitney Balliett), Dixon recalls that they generally didn't get the work, and Newport especially "freaked them out."[37] Although Dixon remembers a "superiorly attentive audience of over 3,000" who met *Pomegranate* "with great enthusiasm," the *New Yorker* jazz critic Whitney Balliett was less enthusiastic: "Bill Dixon presented a dull five-part dirge that was danced to by Judith Dunn, who resembled a melting ice-cream cone."[38]

"Sometimes She Refers to Me as a Dancer"

It would be easy to reduce the rigorous collaborations between Dunn and Dixon to their simplest narrative: white woman abandons the "intellectuality" of charts to dance with "freer" improvising black male musician; or, black male musician "sells out" in playing "dance music" for white woman. But these tropes are too simple and don't do justice to the integrity and the deeply challenging nature of their collaboration. Dunn and Dixon *worked* to be on stage together, striving against the grain of their disciplines and historical expectations—regarding the ways in which men and women should behave, interracial partnerships, the power relations between musicians and dancers, and the status of their respective forms—to engage in rigorous, improvisational ensemble. Although they prioritized their work as artists and thought deeply about the artistic traditions from which they came and their attendant conventions, the improvisational choices they made were never merely about form. How could they have been? As Dixon recently explained, "Collaboration was not just a word. Every detail of our work was discussed. It was a way of life."[39] Perhaps most important, their view of collaboration allowed for disagreement and struggle, both of which were present in their relationship. According to Dunn, "It [collaboration] involves constant effort and a continuing critical attention to the processes involved, both artistic and social."[40] Moreover, Dunn's move from charts and chance procedures certainly was not a romanticized move to instinct. The improvisations Dunn and Dixon embarked upon involved immense training, discipline, and a keen sense of order. Dixon explains: "Everything did not go. Everything was not acceptable. One didn't just huff, take another deep breath of air and blow."[41]

The duo's training process was often as challenging as the work itself, with the two developing an improvisational way of working not just through studio time but through sustained sessions spent listening and talking about the improvisations of Duke Ellington, John Coltrane, Eric Dolphy, and Cecil Taylor. Listening to records and live performances became an important kind of training for both their musical and their danced improvisations. Dunn and Dixon also read from the German series *Der Rhie* and *Jazz Review*.[42] While one might imagine that this impulse came solely from Dixon, Dunn had long possessed a keen musical sensibility. She introduced Dixon to the work of Anton Webern, recognizing similarities between their musical ideas, and influenced Dixon's way of playing. Dixon recalls: "Rhythmically, no one could move the way that she did. There was an instinctive understanding of how the time was passing and just how much one could sub-divide and at the same time use rubato. . . . I viewed, or heard every movement that she did as a sound."[43] Dunn also played guitar, flute, and piano and, according to Dixon, "could sing beautifully those folk and other songs out of the sixties repertoire that I literally hated."[44] Despite their differences, they valued each other's opinions, and throughout their studies of improvised music, the two persistently asked: "How did all of this / if it did / apply to dance movement? And should it, as a philosophy, also apply to dance movement?"[45]

In the early years of American modern dance, choreographers such as Isadora Duncan, Ruth St. Denis, and Louis Fuller strove to make music visible or else to express themselves with music as their aid, two slightly different notions that each elevated the importance of music above dance. While these early choreographers danced primarily in time with the music—being percussive when the music was percussive, lyrical when the music suggested lyricism—their successors began to dance in contrast to the music or independently of it. On October 20, 1957, Paul Taylor gave a performance analogous to John Cage's 4'33", in which the pianist David Tudor sat at the piano without playing a single note. Taylor offered stillness as the equivalent of silence, standing still for the entire dance.[46] There was virtually no visible motion or rhythm, except of course for the vigorous movement and agitation that occurred within the audience. Performances such as this influenced Dunn, along with her years spent working for Cunningham, whose work with Cage further dismantled what many people considered a necessary relationship between dance and music. As evidenced by archival works from the Bennington days, Cunningham had a striking influence on Dunn's choreography. In Dunn's *Summerdance* (1971), the dancers' articulate attention to shape is clearly Cunninghamesque and not at all pedestrian in the Judson manner. But even more significant is their rhythmic sensibility, marked by a confident embrace of stillness and silence.

Before collaborating with Dixon, Dunn performed most of her work in silence or else to the sounds of performers moving.[47] Although Dunn began to perform with music once she met Dixon, she explains that the relationship between music and dance differs from the traditional one-to-one correspondence, wherein "leaps are indicated by ascending arpeggios and falls by thudding chords."[48] Together, Dunn and Dixon strove to create a situation where neither the music nor the dance was subordinate to the other. This dynamic was a live issue in the history of Western concert dance, bound with dancers' struggle for autonomy and legitimacy in the art world. It was also a concern in the masculine world of bebop and improvised music, where musicians resisted being reduced to playing mere "dance music." For example, when asked by Dixon and Dunn to play in their Newport performance, the drummer Sunny Murray responded perfunctorily that he didn't want to play "behind no dancer."[49] Audiences were also resistant, demanding that Dunn and Dixon explain their "competence to 'invade' each other's field."[50]

Still, Dixon and Dunn strove for an ensemblic relation. According to Dixon, their collaboration was "rooted in the idea that both the music and the dance were special and one shouldn't necessarily be used as a subordinate to, or at the expense of the artistic and historical integrity of the other."[51] Although both artists recognized that music and dance have distinct histories and offer unique forms of expression, they recognized "empathy" between their traditions, frequently elided in histories of the New York avant-garde. Dixon explains, "There was a kind of artistic empathy emanating out of the Judson Movement even though the reasons and the methods might, in so many instances, have been diametrically opposed in philosophical terms."[52] In Dixon's view, he and the musicians he admired (such as Taylor, Coltrane, and Ellington) strove to surround themselves with musical environments of their own making—worlds in which they wanted to live. They dedicated themselves to creating music rather than merely imitating the sounds that press upon one's daily life without invitation. This is what made improvisation so important, and it required tremendous commitment and skill. Informed by this sensibility, both Dixon and Dunn believed that they had to take chances. They had to be daring. And they had to do improvisational work in which they believed.[53]

As Dixon and Dunn pursued this politically charged and forward-looking work, their collaborations revealed that improvised music and dance have more in common than typical discussions allow. Dixon explains: "I think of Judy Dunn as a player. Sometimes she refers to me as a dancer."[54] While this statement might seem like a mere nod of respect, the interesting cross-identification between Dunn and Dixon suggests a way of rethinking both improvised music and dance. While dance is obviously an art of the body, Dixon and Dunn understood that musical expression is also bound with gesture. Once, during a rehearsal in the mid-1960s when Dunn had an injury and could barely move, she affixed a variety of trinkets to her body, ranging from bracelets to bells to strings of beads, examining how her limited movements caused the objects to emit sound.[55] Here, Dunn's primary objective was movement. But gesture also affects even the most traditional music. For example, the way one drags one's bow across a violin affects its volume, and the way the instrument touches one's shoulder affects its resonance. Similarly, whether a pianist's note sounds sharp or muted, short or sustained, depends upon the way he or she presses upon the keys.

John Martin made a similar argument back in 1931–32, in the lecture series he delivered at the New School for Social Research. In his talks, Martin analyzed American modern dance, which was still an unfamiliar subject to the general public. Discussing the relation between dance and the other arts, Martin noted that encyclopedias, aesthetic treatises, and even dancers denounce dance as a secondary art that developed out of music. Martin argued, however, that this widespread notion was false. To prove his point, he discussed the relationship between musical sound and gesture:

> So far as I can discover there has never been a sound made in the universe that was not made by movement. Musical sound, especially, is traceable to movement, and even more than that, to muscular movement, to bodily movement. It makes no difference whether it is the sound produced by forcing wind through the vocal cords and resonance chambers of the body or of especially made pipes, or whether it is sound produced by the scraping or plucking of strings, or by striking resounding surfaces of one sort or another.[56]

Despite the force of Martin's argument, his lectures at the New School did little to "break down the patronizing attitude of music and its practitioners."[57]

Thirty-five years after Martin argued that all musical sound comes from bodily movement, Dixon used the same insight to counter the claim that free jazz is an "angry" music. According to Dixon, the physical aggression necessary to create a sustained "angry" sound cannot occur in the physical contact specific to all instruments. He explains, "Unless one was a drummer / where one beats *upon* something / it is virtually impossible to maintain the control and contact with the instrument and one's own physicality necessary to *overtly* project anger via musical performance."[58] Of course, one can play the drums in a variety of ways, creating gentle, shimmering sounds if one desires to do so. And one can make a trumpet scream. Still, Dixon's comment suggests that sound emerges out of gesture—that music exists as a trace, or perhaps extension, of the body's action.

Even though Dixon recognized the corporeality of musical improvisation early on in his collaborations with Dunn, his willingness to move as a dancer only extended so far. As Dixon and Dunn became better adept at improvising together, more in sync with each other's goals and politics, they still had disagreements. One source of contention involved Dixon's reluctance to physically participate in the dance. Dixon maintains that musicians must be comfortable in order to do their world-making work, and for that reason, he didn't want to "physically be part of the movement situation."[59] Photographs of their early collaborations show Dunn dancing around Dixon and other musicians. Although Dixon dismisses these photographs as humorous, they are quite compelling, showing not only the shapes that Dunn made around the players but the relationships of all the bodies to their surrounding environment and to each other. The players' physical relationships with their instruments are particularly interesting. In one photo, taken during a rehearsal for the 1966 Newport performance, Alan Silva stands with legs apart, hunching over his bass, neck craned around his instrument. In another photo, Dixon stands with his horn directed over Dunn's back as she crouches low to the ground with both hands on the floor. Dixon's head is downcast, and his spine and torso are compressed, undoubtedly affecting the flow of air and the sound he emits.

In these photographs, one also sees gender and race, which demands that one think in more complicated ways about Dixon's claim that musicians must be "comfortable" in order to do their difficult improvisatory work.

Dixon's uneasiness resonates with Gavin Bryars's retreat from improvisation, a retreat that was driven by a sense that viewers inevitably identify the music with the visible musician. This issue, however, was particularly salient for black performing artists during the late 1960s. It is of course possible to attribute Dixon's discomfort to numerous factors. Musicians don't typically train with dancers circling them, and it could be dangerous for dancers to move around musicians and their instruments. More important, neither Dunn nor Dixon presumed to be virtuosic in the other's form. Their collaborations were not about dancers mocking musicians or vice versa. They respected each other's extensive training and the particular skills they had acquired. They were not interested in "movement situations" that looked sloppy, or cliché, or like bad performance art.[60] Still, it's hard to discuss Dixon's reluctance to "be part of the dance" without at least considering his 1967 claim about visibility: "It's quite obvious, (if I'm seen) . . . that I'm playing out of a so-called black experience. But then again, I'd prefer someone to say that I'm playing out of my own experience."[61] The parenthetical "if I'm seen" screams in its ambivalent, hesitant admission. He'd prefer that the situation be otherwise. The point here is that visual pathologies such as racism sometimes make it uncomfortable (if not outright dangerous in certain situations) for people of color to "participate" in highly visible improvisations. For Dixon in the late 1960s, the legibility that comes with his being seen limits the possible reception of his music: a significant burden. As I've said earlier, improvisation doesn't always provide identical resistance for everyone involved, and sometimes one person's "freedom" exacerbates another person's discomfort.

It's unfortunate that no written record exists of Dunn's reasons for wanting the musicians to participate more fully in the "movement situation." Despite significant contributions to her field—as teacher, dancer, and choreographer/improviser—both Robert Dunn and Dixon eclipse Judith Dunn in history books. Although Dunn engaged in rigorous collaborations with both men, she died of a brain tumor in 1983, and her partners' published statements far exceed her own. Perhaps she knew that the musicians' sounds were bound with gesture in ways not entirely unlike improvised dance—that musicians' aural improvisations were always already corporeal whether or not they wanted to imagine them as such. Perhaps she understood that an ensemblic relation wherein neither dance nor music was subordinate to the other depended upon a "shared space." Perhaps she understood the political and historical significance, fraught and occasionally uncomfortable, of a Judson dancer and a free jazz musician, one white and one black, one female and one male, publicly sharing improvised space, neither behind the other.

Dianne McIntyre: "Boom, Boom, Boom, Dah, Dah"

Although Judith Dunn and Bill Dixon were significant in their own right, they also helped to inspire the investigations of Dianne McIntyre, another young dancer who built upon their legacy and continued to challenge the racial and gender divisions within the worlds of improvised music and dance. In 1972, McIntyre formed her own ensemble of musicians and dancers called Sounds in Motion.[62] In many ways, McIntyre emerged out of the same tradition as Dunn, receiving similar modern dance training. But as a black woman, she fit into that tradition differently. Born in Cleveland in 1946, McIntyre began taking ballet and tap lessons at the age of four. Although her first teacher was white, most of the students were black. Interestingly, in an act of deep disidentification—a concept José Muñoz develops as an oppositional mode of reception where minoritarian subjects (often as a means of survival) creatively refashion mainstream identities and cultural icons—McIntyre powerfully created and believed in a black Martha Graham.[63] McIntyre recalls: "I don't know, I thought modern dance was really like a black art form. Just a couple here and there, a white person might be kind of interested in it. . . . I even thought back then that Martha Graham was black."[64] She continues: "I would hear about Graham. Yes. I may even have seen a picture of her, but it didn't matter. I saw maybe a fuzzy picture of her, but I still thought she might be just a light-skinned black person."[65]

As a black woman training as a dancer in the 1950s and 1960s, McIntyre transformed pictures of Martha Graham, in many ways the white diva of modern dance, into something *useful*. This powerful mode of reception resembles James Baldwin's encounter with the white actress Bette Davis, as described in Baldwin's extended essay *The Devil Finds Work*. Gazing at the white female actress during a Saturday matinee, emanating from the screen with her big eyes and glasses of champagne, Baldwin explains, "I gave Davis's skin the dead white greenish cast of something crawling from under a rock, but I was held, just the same, by the tense intelligence of the forehead, the disaster of the lips: and when she moved, she moved just like a nigger."[66] According to Muñoz, Baldwin's response to Davis constitutes a quintessential example of disidentification: "The example of Baldwin's relationship with Davis is a disidentification in so far as the African-American writer transforms the raw material of identification (the linear match that leads toward interpellation) while simultaneously positioning himself within and outside the image of the movie star."[67] For both McIntyre and Baldwin, disidentification proved to be not merely a fanciful act of imagination, but an important survival strategy. For McIntyre, by configuring a black Martha Graham, she negotiated a relation to modernism that enabled her to *dance*.

One can imagine McIntyre's surprise when, thinking that modern dance was "our ethnic dance," she enrolled as a dance major at Ohio State University, where she was the only black student. McIntyre recalls: "I was just blown away. I was like, 'And they are good, too.'"[68] McIntyre received a strong technical training at Ohio State, where students were encouraged to choreograph and contribute something "new" to the field, and was introduced to Dunn and Dixon during her college years. Clearly inspired by their work, McIntyre explains that she appreciated the duo's improvisational principles and the unconventional relationship they espoused between music and dance. Recalling her first exposure to Dunn and Dixon, McIntyre explains: "I loved that, their connection. . . . [Dunn] gave us principles of improvisation that were very broad, that didn't have stylistic background to them, so that we could take the improv into whatever. Yes, I got inspired by that there, the improv."[69] Although McIntyre briefly studied improvisation with Dunn and Dixon in college, she explains that she eventually went to great lengths to distinguish her work from theirs, which she described as exceedingly intellectual. She strove to establish an even deeper ensemblic connection between musicians and dancers, which would surpass a relationship of merely "sharing space."[70]

McIntyre graduated from Ohio State University and moved to New York in 1970, where she studied with Viola Farber, Alwin Nikolais, and Gus Solomons Jr. Influenced by the U.S. civil rights era and the Black Arts Movement, McIntyre was committed to forming a company of black dancers upon moving to New York. She remembers thinking: "It's going to be a force, an energy, behind what we do, but it's going to be as creative as possible. I've always felt like we've grown up in this culture, so we're trained in traditional, classical, European ways, in modern dance ways. We have our own expression from our background and social dance. So all those can come through, but I didn't want to repeat some things that are thought of as the dance that black people do."[71] Valuing innovation and desiring artistic autonomy, McIntyre didn't want to be limited by reductive notions of blackness or black dance. She wanted to incorporate both her modern dance training and a tradition of social dance, hoping to arrive at something culturally and historically honest. McIntyre explains, "I felt that if I couldn't do all that stuff from the '30s and '40s, then what I'd be doing in a freer form wouldn't be honest."[72] So, in addition to studio training, McIntyre studied social dance forms with a number of dancers who had frequented Harlem's Savoy Ballroom during its heyday in the 1930s, learning improvisational principles like the "break," as well as exploring possible relations between music and dance. Studying social dances such as the lindy, jitterbug, cakewalk, and Charleston, McIntyre investigated an improvised tradition of social dance never approached by Judith Dunn, despite its deep relationship with jazz.

McIntyre's training in social dance is evident in her work. When improvising, she frequently breaks into shimmies, hip-shakes, or even quick struts that one would likely see in a dance hall. In 1972, she choreographed *Smoke and Clouds,* which contained pockets of improvisation, where dancers could invent their own phrases or group relationships within parameters set by McIntyre. In a clear outgrowth of her training, the piece draws from abstract modern dance moves (with extended limbs, clear shapes, and a dramatic sense of timing) and social dance idioms (with hip-shaking, stomping, and casual walking around the space). Similarly, the music alternates among recorded rock-and-roll, live conga drumming, and vocalization by the dancers. *Smoke and Clouds* begins with couples dancing a slow dance in a typical embrace, swaying back and forth to the beat of "Come on baby let the good times roll," sung by Shirley and Lee. At that point, the recorded music stops abruptly as the dancers fall to the ground. Then, in a scene that challenges the seemingly carefree world of social dance, the dancers get up, screaming, and cluster toward the corner. Live conga drumming begins, as the dancers strike out with bold moves diagonally across the stage. Different idioms overlap each other throughout the piece, interrupting each other, challenging each other, mixing the worlds of "high" and "low" art. Knowing her history, McIntyre comes from all these places.

In addition to studying social dance, McIntyre immersed herself in the free jazz or new music scene during her first years in New York. She listened to as much as she could and knew that she wanted to work with musicians. McIntyre frequented places like The East in Brooklyn, a black cultural center that was a school by day and a club in the evenings and on weekends. At The East, she heard Gary Bartz and Pharaoh Sanders—"all the great ones," according to McIntyre.[73] Listening to this music, she immediately understood its emergence in relation to civil rights struggles. According to McIntyre, "[The music] was very expressive of the feeling of that time, that freedom, just breaking through with freedom. The musicians who were the most brilliant in that area, you could really soar on the music."[74] Soon after moving to New York, McIntyre came into contact with a collective group of musicians called the Master Brotherhood, a 1970s name that suggests the extent to which free jazz and notions of blackness were equated with masculinity. The group included Ahmed Abdullah, Joe Rigby, Arthur Williams, Mustafa Abdul Rahim, Les Walker, Joe Falcon, and Steve Reid.

Forging an opening in this male world, McIntyre asked the group if she could attend their rehearsals, explaining that she wanted to think critically about the relations between improvised music and dance. Joining the musicians' rehearsals in a Brooklyn day-care center, a space that complicates visions of a "master brotherhood," McIntyre began by moving aside the children's playthings, so she could dance while the musicians played. Initially, she tried to make her body move like the music sounded. She explains: "I would do it over and over again, and sometimes I was doing some things that seemed almost impossible. It was very invigorating."[75] Attempting to learn from the structures and gestural impulses within free jazz, McIntyre explains: "There are certain things they (Jazz musicians) do in runs that are intricate and very very fast. I hadn't seen parallel things in movement."[76]

But, as with Dunn's collaboration with Dixon, McIntyre's relation to the music quickly went beyond mere emulation. Before long, McIntyre began to feel like another instrument, and she and the musicians developed a back-and-forth rapport where they influenced each other. McIntyre invited four musicians from the Master Brotherhood, along with four dancers, to be a part of her first New York performance, entitled *A Free Thing*, which was totally improvised. McIntyre explains: "It had absolutely no structure. But those first people I worked with, Bill, Bernadine, Dorian, and myself, in that time, we could improvise and the musicians could, where we could make structure as we were going."[77] The dancers and musicians rigorously rehearsed for this performance, knowing the importance of spontaneously created structure. The freedom in *A Free Thing* was certainly more than "one's happy hour."

In 1972, McIntyre founded Sounds in Motion, which employed both musicians and dancers. Initially, the company rehearsed in a Harlem office building called the Ministerial Interfaith Association, as well as Harlem's Studio Museum. But in 1978, Sounds in Motion moved into its own studio on 125th Street and Lenox Avenue. While McIntyre worked with numerous musicians over the course of her career, Cecil Taylor was her most consistent early collaborator. They first worked together in 1974, creating an improvised tribute to Syvilla Fort, a well-known dancer from the Katherine Dunham Dance Company. In rehearsals, they quickly developed a rapid back-and-forth process where both Taylor and the dancers took cues from each other, attentively listening to and watching each other's improvisations. McIntyre recalls: "Work with Cecil was totally cyclical. It was all coming at the same time: fast and furious."[78] Perhaps more than other musicians, Cecil Taylor had a dancer's sensibility and was able to recognize and remember sequences of movement. As McIntyre fondly recalls: "Cecil was a very, very dance-oriented person. He knew dance back from, he would tell us back in 1940 dah, dah, dah, he saw the original ballet at the boom, boom, boom, dah, dah."[79] For McIntyre and Taylor, improvised dance was intensely intellectual and bound with an understanding of social dance history. Perhaps most important, the rapid, improvised exchanges that occurred between the musicians and dancers who worked within Sounds in Motion engendered a radical understanding of embodied ensemble. According to McIntyre, "It was like Cecil and I and the dancers, we all came into be like one body."[80]

Sounds in Motion expanded upon Judith Dunn and Bill Dixon's interesting cross-identification, where Dixon viewed Dunn as a "player" and Dunn viewed Dixon as a dancer. McIntyre's collaborations with free jazz musicians, which emerged out of a deep love for the music and a vested interest in the era's black radicalism, resulted in critical insight regarding the corporeality of improvisation. McIntyre explains: "As I went on and on, I realized that music was so special to me that the dance actually was the music, so that the dancer's body became a musical instrument. So it began more and more to merge with the music, and I found that there is no difference between the dancer and the music.'"[81] McIntyre understood the importance of expanding one's sensual awareness.

The presentation of this full, improvising body had political implications regarding race, but also gender. As noted earlier, McIntyre's work challenged the notion of a "master brotherhood." Still, most of the musicians with

whom McIntyre collaborated during the formative years of Sounds in Motion were male—Cecil Taylor, Butch Morris, Doug Hammond, Ahmed Abdullah, and Olu Dara. When asked recently whether she was aware of gender during her early collaborations with musicians—whether her being a
woman affected dynamics within the ensemble—McIntyre agreed that she
worked primarily with male musicians during the 1970s, although there were
a few exceptions: Sharon Freeman (a pianist and french hornist), Amina
Claudine Myers (a pianist and vocal composer/arranger), and Gwendolyn
Nelson Fleming (a vocalist), who was a part of Sounds in Motion from the
very beginning. After noting these female musicians, McIntyre explained, "I
was enamored by the music, and wasn't really thinking about gender at the
time." Still, she noted that, because there was very little precedent for the ensemblic work she was doing, getting the musicians on board required a certain degree of "diplomacy." Few of the musicians had worked with dance.
According to McIntyre, "There might have been a bit of male dominance,
but I didn't think about it in those terms at the time."

Before long, however, memories began to flow, and McIntyre recounted
an instance where gender played a big role. It involved a duet with a male
drummer, whom McIntyre declined to name. The two had rehearsed together
for hours, developing a plan for their upcoming performance. Like much of
McIntyre's work, it would be a structured improvisation, determined mostly
by energy, tempo, and rhythmic concerns. Although rehearsals were great,
the drummer adopted an intensity in performance that had been entirely absent in rehearsals. According to McIntyre, he didn't pay attention to anything
she was doing (the antithesis of ensemblic improvisation); instead, he sat
there, laughing as he aggressively pounded upon his instrument. McIntyre re-
called dancing with her back to the audience, screaming at the musician:
"What are you doing?" She explained that, at the time, they couldn't have
had the same power. He was in charge. McIntyre exclaimed, "It was like he
was trying to beat me down."

The effects of gender on McIntyre's early work were far-reaching, even in
performances far less spectacular than the incident described earlier. These
effects certainly aren't reducible to the fact that there were more male musicians in the new music scene than female musicians and more professional
dancers in New York who were women than men (although these differences
certainly deserve to be noted). It is important to reckon with the fact that
McIntyre felt she didn't have access to the same power that the male drum-

mer drew upon. It is also important to think about form. Although McIntyre's ensemble shared space and developed vibrant improvisational exchanges during rehearsals, performances typically occurred in conventional
settings with the musicians offstage and the dancers visually framed, front
and center. The musicians were heard, and the dancers were seen. McIntyre
departed from these gendered conventions, however, in a performance with
Abbey Lincoln, a radical performer who greatly expanded the role of the
black female vocalist. The performance was neither famous nor well docu-
mented. But the deeply embodied practice evidenced in the work is important
to consider. According to McIntyre, dancing with Lincoln for the first time
was a "magical" experience.

The Freedom Now Suite

Born Anna Marie Wooldridge in Chicago, in 1930, Lincoln was raised in
Michigan. Moving to Los Angeles in 1954, she assumed a variety of stage
names as she built a career as a sultry supper club singer, who was billed as a
black version of white sex symbols, most notably Marilyn Monroe. During
the mid-1950s, she changed her name from Anna Marie, to Gaby
Wooldridge, to the popular Gaby Lee. *Ebony* introduced the young star to its
public, exclaiming, "The hottest new singer to hit Hollywood this season is a
tall, shapely, torch-voiced lass who is billed as Miss Gaby Lee."[82] Not long
afterward, in 1957, *Ebony* presented a series of photographs with Lincoln
clad in famous dresses of Marilyn Monroe, imitating many of the blond's
poses. As Farah Jasmine Griffin explains, Lincoln was being groomed for a
particular role, "poised to inherit the mantle of black sex symbol, a browner
version of . . . café au lait chanteuses."[83] Lincoln recalls that, with a repertoire that consisted entirely of love songs, "I didn't yet think of myself as a serious artist or as a serious person either. All I wanted was to be thought of as
beautiful and desirable."[84]

This would soon change. In 1956, at the instigation of her manager, Gaby
Lee changed her name yet again, this time to Abbey Lincoln, in honor of the
country's sixteenth president. The civil rights movement was gaining momentum, and Lincoln found herself diverging from the seemingly simple
chanteuse. "It was the early days of the civil rights movement," Lincoln recalls, "and we were all asking the same questions. But they were questions
that glamour girls weren't supposed to ask. As I toured the country, I noticed

that black people everywhere were living in slums, in abject poverty. I wanted to know why."[85]

Paralleling McIntyre's collaborations with the Master Brotherhood in the 1970s, Abbey Lincoln moved to New York in 1957 and stepped into a scene of politicized black male musicians. She started to write her own lyrics and began to record with Max Roach. In 1959, just as black male musicians began rejecting the term *jazz*, Lincoln embraced the term as offering possibilities for political assertion not otherwise open to black female singers. She explained to *Jet* magazine that year: "I'm a black woman, and I have to sing about things I feel and know about—jazz. In the supper clubs something inside me isn't content."[86] Soon after moving to New York, she stopped straightening her hair and stopped visiting her voice coach, with whom she had worked to remove her "Negro" intonation.[87]

Expanding the role of the female jazz vocalist, Lincoln committed herself to socially conscious songs and adopted an increasingly instrumental approach to singing. She experimented with timbre and vocal technique and participated in Roach's musical arrangements much like the other players. While this move toward instrument widened Lincoln's range of vocal expression (moving away from lyrics toward abstract sound), it also opened up an increasingly participatory role for the female vocalist within the male-dominated world of jazz ensemble. As noted by Eric Porter, one can trace Lincoln's shift by comparing three consecutive Riverside recordings, all made in the late 1950s: *That's Him* (1957), *It's Magic* (1958), and *Abbey Is Blue* (1959). In these albums, the influence of Billie Holiday's timing and self-assured approach to lyrics becomes more apparent. In addition, the songs Lincoln selects increasingly show signs of the black freedom movement, engaging with social problems beyond those that occur within romantic relationships. Although *That's Him* contains mostly love songs and standards, Lincoln presents sorrowful tales about injustice in *Abbey Is Blue*. This stark album contains a song called "Lonely House," with lyrics from a Langston Hughes poem about loneliness and urban alienation, as well as "Let Up," a fourteen-bar blues with lyrics written by Lincoln herself.[88] Midway through this song, Lincoln repeats the phrase "ease up" three times and then plaintively asks, "When will trouble ease up? How much can a body abide?"

In the late summer of 1960, Lincoln performed the vocals for *We Insist! The Freedom Now Suite*. The drummer Max Roach and the lyricist Oscar Brown Jr. intended this work to commemorate the centennial of Abraham

Lincoln's 1862 Emancipation Proclamation. However, fueled by the 1960 student sit-ins, Roach created a shorter version to express solidarity with the civil rights movement. First recorded in the fall of 1960, the album featured the Nigerian drummer Michael Olatunji and the tenor saxophonist Coleman Hawkins, in addition to Roach, Brown, and Lincoln. The group publicly performed the suite for the first time at New York's Village Gate in 1961, sponsored by the Congress on Racial Equality (CORE).[89] In this performance, Lincoln exploded expectations regarding "song" and conventional comportment for the female "singer," screaming and wailing rather than merely singing lyrics. Her experimentation with vocal range reached an unprecedented dynamism in "Triptych: Prayer/Protest/Peace," a duet for Lincoln and Roach that constitutes the powerful middle section of the five-part *Freedom Now Suite*.

Even recordings of "Triptych" can be harrowing, pulling the listener through the arc of the work. Although "Prayer" begins with sparse, steady runs of a snare drum, Lincoln's voice then emerges, projecting a wordless spiritual over and around Roach's accompaniment. Her voice pushes out in deeply resonant tones, emitting round sounds, full of undulation. Direct, purposeful wails waft out from deep cavities. "Protest" then pierces this resonant prayer as Lincoln begins to scream. The drumming picks up with crashing symbols and furious rolls. Again and again, she screams. Shrill, urgent sounds shoot through her throat, like there is not enough space. But they extend outward, piercing everything in their path. Each shriek evokes rape, witness, passage, horror, murder, protest, song. But Lincoln's voice returns to a lower register in "Peace." With deep sighs and ample breath, the work concludes as Lincoln's lilting voice streams over a steady rhythmic pulse. Roach describes this final section as "the feeling of relaxed exhaustion after you've done everything you can to assert yourself. You can rest now because you've worked to be free."[90]

The Freedom Now Suite offers a keen articulation of protest, inseparable from Lincoln's screams. Lincoln maintains that screaming "freed her up," attributing this to the male musicians with whom she worked, most notably Max Roach, whom she married in 1962 and divorced in 1970. Their relationship, however, was both inspiring and frequently brutal. Moreover, both formal and social constraints remained well after Lincoln learned how to scream. "Freedom" is not a destination one reaches once and for all. Lincoln recalls, "[Roach] was willing to give me everything as long as I did what he said."[91] Elsewhere, she recalls, "Max and I were divorced in 1970 and I was like a wounded animal." She then checked herself into a psychiatric hospital for five weeks.[92] As much as Lincoln's screams exorcised pain and projected urgent protest, they doubled back and took a psychic and bodily toll. Lincoln damaged her vocal chords in the performance of "Protest."[93] It hurts to scream like that.

The more one listens, the more one realizes that there's no easy division between art and life in *The Freedom Now Suite*. Although one could talk about screaming in musical terms, its significance is inextricable from the social world and its various constraints. This becomes particularly clear in Fred Moten's improvised notes, taken during a Jazz Study Group interview with Abbey Lincoln in 1999:

> I was born the tenth of twelve children. . . . / I visited a psychiatric hospital 'cause Roach said there was madness in the house. He said it wasn't him, so I figured it must be me / they had me hollering and screaming like a crazy person; I ain't hollering and screaming for my freedom. The women I come from will take something and knock you. . . . / Monk whispered in my ear, "Don't be so perfect." He meant make a mistake; reach for something / I didn't think a scream was part of the music / We were riding in the car with my nephew who was eight years old and who said "The reason I can scream louder than Aunt Abbey is 'cause I'm a little boy" / Went all over the world hollering and screaming. . . . I got rid of a taboo and screamed in everybody's face / We had to go to court; somebody thought Roach was killing me in the studio / My instrument is deepening and widening. . . . It's holy work and it's dangerous not to know that 'cause you could die like an animal down here.[94]

Moten explains that his notes are "a recording, an improvisation, of her [Lincoln's] words, troubled by the trace of the performance of which she tells and the performance of which that performance told."[95] Moten's passage of "improvised notes" has an undeniable intensity. The words spill onto the page, where some sentences break abruptly and others trail off unfinished. Perhaps an improvisation on Lincoln's words, crafted with attention to form and flow, is the only way that writing could approach the feeling of her performance. Regardless, this improvisational recording makes it clear that the sound of Lincoln's "music," the "holy work" of her screaming, is bound with real-life horror that is racialized, gendered, sexualized, and frequently played out on the body. Immediately after Lincoln states that people thought Roach was killing her in the studio, she claims that her instrument—her voice, her body—is widening. As if an "instrumental widening," which has everything to do with Lincoln's body, could justify the pain.

In the last chapter of *If You Can't Be Free, Be a Mystery,* referring to the same presentation discussed by Moten, Farah Jasmine Griffin quotes Lincoln as explaining, "I'm not the kind of woman that screams. I tried, and I couldn't scream."[96] Despite these early feelings, Lincoln's experience with her nephew, and Monk, and Roach, and a whole lot of pain eventually led her to begin screaming, and she has been doing so ever since. But what does it mean to be "the *kind of woman* that screams"? The very fact that such a category exists, one from which a younger Lincoln had wanted to distance herself, shows the gendered significance of Lincoln's urgent sound. On the one hand, it's what makes and signifies a woman as "crazy." But on the other hand, as Lincoln maintains, "It's part of the protection of a woman that she can scream."[97]

New Dance: Prayer, Protest, Peace

In the summer of 1980, two decades after *The Freedom Now Suite*'s original recording and eight years after the formation of Sounds in Motion, Dianne McIntyre presented two evenings of performance at New York's Symphony Space entitled *New Dance.* Each night, she performed collaborative works with different musicians: the first night featured the saxophonists Oliver Lake and Hamiett Bluett, while the second night featured the saxophonist Gary Bartz and the trumpeter Ahmed Abdullah. But the centerpiece of both evenings was McIntyre's collaboration with Roach and Lincoln, in a performance both haunting and righteous. Together, the trio performed "Triptych: Prayer, Protest, Peace." While *The Freedom Now Suite* is inextricably linked with the civil rights movement, Lincoln explained that the album's message still applied in 1980, when she participated in McIntyre's *New Dance* concert. "The protest isn't over," she said. "*The Freedom Now Suite* and what it stands for are as valid as they were then."[98]

Insisting upon the ongoing validity of *The Freedom Now Suite,* Lincoln draws attention to shifting yet persistent social ills such as racism and sexism. But, intertwined with this challenge to explicit social strictures, their protest also bears upon restrictive understandings of music and dance. These are some of the tight places with which their work engaged. As seen in rehearsal photographs, McIntyre is lean and long-limbed, with narrow hips and broad shoulders. She wears dark tights and a three-quarter-sleeve leotard, typical dance attire for 1980, showing lines and curves and slight motions of the body, including the dancer's breath. There's something fierce and austere in McIntyre's bodily exposure, a far cry from the Marilyn Monroe dresses that Lincoln modeled in the 1950s. McIntyre's hair is pulled back in a headscarf, and while clearly dressed for dancing, she is also dressed for work. Performing together for the first time in eleven years, Lincoln and Roach stand on either side of McIntyre, clad in street clothes. While their bodily positions are not as extreme or symmetrical as McIntyre's, one can imagine the sounds they emit as they move, especially knowing the *Freedom Now* score. An urgent sound animates these photographs.

In keeping with McIntyre's philosophy, the 1980 performance of "Triptych: Prayer, Protest, Peace" moved beyond the relationship whereby only Lincoln and Roach provided heard sound and only McIntyre provided a seen body. According to McIntyre, her dancing in "Prayer" was clear and choreographed, even reverential. She felt supported by Lincoln's voice, even as it pushed her into the next place. In contrast, "Protest" was explosive and almost entirely improvised. Dancing to it was "very, very hard." Although McIntyre recalls jumping and falling to the ground during "Protest," frequently bruising herself in the process, the tone of her voice in a recent conversation suggests that this "hardness" transcended mere scrapes and bruises. It also had something to do with the social-historical weight of Lincoln's sound. According to McIntyre, although her relationship with Lincoln during the performance of "Protest" was hard, it differed dramatically from her experience with the male drummer who attempted to "beat her down." Occasionally, McIntyre would move close to Lincoln (whose ability to travel across the space was limited by her microphone's cord), relating to her as another dancer. "Peace," the final section of the work, was much calmer. McIntyre explains: "It was real. What do you have to do to come back to your center? We found this from each other."

Evidence of this complexity exists even in the few published reviews of the performance, which (in unusual fashion) acknowledged dancerly aspects of Roach and Lincoln's performance, while also noting McIntyre's musical approach. According to Linda Small, "[Lincoln] wrenches horrifying screams from her soul, actually rearing back and shaking the sounds out of her body.

Figure 4. Dianne McIntyre, Abbey Lincoln, and Max Roach rehearsing for "Tryptich" in 1980. Photo by Laura Levine.

McIntyre explodes and flails as Roach creates a military drum roll overlaid with irregular, gunshot-like accents."[99] While Small describes the ways in which Lincoln and Roach "danced," Julinda Lewis Williams notes the musicality within McIntyre's motion: "As [Lincoln]'s voice sighs and screams into the microphone and golden lights bounce off Max Roach's drums, McIntyre flings herself about, gliding on the notes and translating the rhythms into different parts [of] her body."[100] As the reviewers attest, the performance magnified relationships between Lincoln's screams and her moving body, shaking and wrenching to release sound. As for Roach, even though his instrument differs from voice, his militaristic drum rolls also emerge out of gesture. And while McIntyre's body illustrates complex rhythmic structures, it becomes clear that her body also has interior space and the capacity to scream. In this unique performance, the three performers pushed with and against each other, screaming and moving in a full-bodied articulation of protest.

The Problem with Pleasure

This chapter has focused on two sets of improvisational collaborations: Judith Dunn's work with Bill Dixon and Dianne McIntyre's work with various musicians. Although these projects were distinct in many ways, both ventures in improvisation resisted restrictive claims that dance is an art of the body while music is an art of the mind, a notion that pervades mainstream American culture as well as discussions of improvisation and much of Western critical theory.[101] Roland Barthes, a French social and literary theorist, provides an interesting exception to this bias. Although Barthes never writes about dance or improvisation explicitly, the force of McIntyre's claim that "there is no difference between the dancer and the music" reverberates throughout his work.[102] In much of his writing from the 1970s—"The Grain of the Voice," *The Pleasure of the Text,* and several of the essays anthologized in *The Responsibility of Forms*—Barthes searches for traces of the artist's body, whether in novels, paintings, or musical recordings.

Barthes's search for the body begs certain questions of ethical reception— for example, how ought one receive the performing bodies in this chapter, particularly when searching for them through scant archives, well after the fact of their performance? By turning to questions of reception in the following pages, I do not mean to suggest that the improvisations under discussion in this chapter were powerful principally because of their legibility or the breadth of their effect. None of these works was famous. As discussed in the introduction, this book explores improvisation as a vital technology of the self and is therefore primarily concerned with *practice*. Still, as I hope the performances in this chapter have made clear, issues of practice and reception are often inextricably linked. Acts of beholding can create the tightest kinds of spaces, and one would be remiss not to consider the contexts in which dancing occurs and the effects that different modes of spectatorship have upon one's ability to improvise.

In his essay "The Grain of the Voice," Barthes develops the concept of grain to designate "the body in the singing voice, in the writing hand, in the performing limb."[103] Although Barthes begins the essay by discussing song, he claims that grain persists even in instrumental music, where it is also possible to detect the artist's body. According to Barthes:

> I hear without a doubt—the certitude here of the body, of the body's enjoyment—that Wanda Landowska's harpsichord comes from her inner

body, and not from the minor digital knitting of so many harpsichordists (to the point where I hear a different instrument); and with regard to piano music, I know immediately which part of the body it is that plays: if it is the arms, as all too often it is, muscular as a dancer's calf, or the talons (regardless of the wrist flourishes), or if on the contrary it is the only erotic part of a pianist's body: the pads of the fingers, whose "grain" I hear so rarely.[104]

In this quotation, Barthes makes several claims that relate to the work of Dunn, Dixon, and McIntyre. By assuming that a dancer's calf is muscular, he recognizes that technique affects the performer's body. Barthes also asserts that one can hear the body in instrumental music. According to Barthes, one can hear the shape, motion, and texture of a musician's body, even territory that exists beneath the skin's surface—the tongue, the glottis, the sinuses, the lungs. He then argues that listening for grain might enable a new form of musical evaluation that, while individual, would transcend the typical pronouncements: "I like" or "I don't like." He explains, "I am determined to listen to my relation to the body of someone who is singing or playing."[105]

He takes a similar approach to literature. In *The Pleasure of the Text*, Barthes tries to create an active role for the reader, while at the same time preserving some degree of the text's autonomy. He therefore decides to judge texts according to his own pleasure. He explains:

If I agree to judge a text according to pleasure, I cannot go on to say: this one is good, that bad. No awards, no "critique," for this always implies a tactical aim, a social usage, and frequently an extenuating image-reservoir. I cannot apportion, imagine that the text is perfectible, ready to enter into a play of normative predicates: it is too much *this,* not enough *that;* the text (the same is true of the singing voice) can wring from me only this judgment, in no way adjectival: *that's it!* And further still: *that's it for me!*[106]

There is an ethical imperative at work here. Barthes doesn't want to misuse the text for social purposes, or reduce its complexity through adjectival description.

In "Cy Twombly: Works on Paper," one recognizes that pleasure, but also agony, propels Barthes's search for the body amid traces. Just as Barthes hears grain in certain pianists, or in Wanda Landowska's harpsichord, he relates lines in painting to the artist's body. He explains that a line is the visible remnant of an action, the trace of an artist's direction and physical expenditure.[107] Barthes then spends an entire morning perusing an anthology of Cy Twombly's work, trying to imitate the artist's gestures. He explains, "I very slowly look through a book of TW's [Twombly's] reproductions, and I frequently stop in order to attempt, quite quickly, on slips of paper, to make certain scribbles; I am not directly imitating TW (what would be the use of that?), I am imitating his *gesture,* which I, if not unconsciously, at least dreamily, infer from my reading; I am not copying the product, but the producing, I am putting myself, so to speak, *in the hand's footsteps.*"[108] One might say that Barthes is more interested in means than ends—more interested in improvisational gestures (both Twombly's and his own) than the painting-as-object.

For Barthes, the "agreeable" endeavor of emulating Twombly's gestures emerges out of a fatal realization: that "my body will never be yours."[109] To a large extent, Barthes's devastating sense of his own singularity underlies his attempt to imitate Twombly's gestures. He explains, "From this fatality, in which a certain human affliction can be epitomized, there is only one means of escape: seduction: that my body (or its sensuous substitutes, art, writing) seduce, overwhelm, or disturb the other body."[110] Moving in relation to another person's gestures offers Barthes a "means of escape."

Here, a progressive way of approaching an other in performance emerges, where rather than sit back and visually objectify the person on stage, one attempts to join the dance. Barthes's experience with Twombly's drawings resembles what John Martin and others have called a kinesthetic response to bodies in motion. According to Martin, because everyone has a body, people experience "muscular sympathy," even when watching extreme motions that they could never actually perform. He argues: "Through kinesthetic sympathy you respond to the impulse of the dancer which has expressed itself by means of a series of movements. Movement then, is the link between the dancer's intentions and your own perception of it."[111] It is unlikely that one can ever know the dancer's intentions through his or her movements. Still, Martin's argument that kinesthesia offers "sympathy" and a "link" between individuals resembles Barthes's claim that shared gesture offers a way out of solitude.

A more contemporary take on this notion (which avoids the pitfalls of intention and direct communication between unified selves) has emerged in dance scholarship that engages with philosophical discussions of affect. In *Exhausting Dance: Performance and the Politics of Movement,* André

Lepecki urges the field of dance studies "to consider in which ways choreography and philosophy share that same fundamental political, ontological, physiological, and ethical question that Deleuze recuperates from Spinoza and from Neitzsche: what can a body do?"[112] One of the things a body can do is affect another body. At first glance, this may seem like a simple observation. But affectual relationships exist at the heart of recent dance practice and theory, and their ethical ramifications are profound.

Brian Massumi's writings are particularly useful in analyzing possible relations between dance and affect. He explains:

> By "affect" I don't mean "emotion" in the everyday sense. The way I use it comes primarily from Spinoza. He talks of the body in terms of its capacity for affecting or being affected. These are not two different capacities—they always go together. When you affect something, you are at the same time opening yourself up to being affected in turn, and in a slightly different way than you might have been the moment before. You have made a transition, however slight. You have stepped over a threshold. Affect is this passing of a threshold, seen from the point of view of the change in capacity. It's crucial to remember that Spinoza uses this to talk about the body. What a body is, he says, is what it can do as it goes along. This is a totally pragmatic definition. A body is defined by what capacities it carries from step to step. What these are exactly is changing constantly. A body's ability to affect or be affected—its charge of affect—isn't something fixed.[113]

For Massumi, there is a profound relation between the affectual dimensions of one's life and hope, in so far as affect suggests ongoing manouverability and the possibility for experimentation. It's a matter of being where you are, in the present, more intensely and figuring out your next experimental step. One might add that these experimental steps are also necessarily *improvisational*. Still, it is problematic to assume that to "seduce, overwhelm, or disturb the other body" incurs no cost, as Barthes seems to suggest. In Barthes's late writings, his mode of reception increasingly encroaches upon the artist's body, and terms like *desire* and *pleasure* and *ego* supplant humble attempts to approach others through gesture.

In "Visible Music," a chapter from *In the Break: The Aesthetics of the Black Radical Tradition*, Fred Moten makes precisely this point, lambasting Barthes's late work for showcasing a "violent egocentricism" that ignores the historical particularity of objects. Moten makes this argument by discussing

"The Great Family of Man," an essay that Barthes wrote in the 1950s. In the essay, Barthes discusses a photograph of Emmett Till, a fourteen-year-old boy who was taken from his bed, mutilated beyond recognition, and thrown into Mississippi's Tallahatchie River for allegedly whistling at a white woman. Reflecting on the young boy's mangled body, Barthes ponders what Till's parents would have thought about a then-current photography exhibit, *The Great Family of Man*. Imagining the parents' negative response, Barthes criticizes the exhibit's ahistorical, lyrical presentation of "universal" notions of birth and death. Barthes claims that the photo exhibit failed to show historical injustices such as "whether or not the child is born with ease or difficulty, whether or not his birth causes suffering to his mother, whether or not he is threatened with a high mortality rate, whether or not such and such a future is open to him."[114] Barthes then argues that the exhibit should have shown such historical particularities. Presumably thinking of Till, Barthes asks: "Must we really celebrate [death's] essence once more, and thus risk forgetting that there is still so much we can do to fight it? It is this very young, far too young power that we must exalt, and not the sterile identity of 'natural' death."[115]

Moten maintains that this early essay rightly displays a genuine concern for historical specificity and the effects of context when analyzing works of art, but that Barthes's pursuit of personal pleasure in the 1970s deeply compromised this concern. When "The Great Family of Man" was first published in *Mythologies* in 1957, Barthes demanded that one consider the effects of history and difference on works of art. But by the 1970s, his approach had changed significantly. As Barthes attempted to access his own pleasure, his concerns revolved around finding the "it" that existed "for him." Moten's critique of Barthes's late rejection of historicity is important to keep in mind when considering romantic discussions of affect in dance. It reminds us, once again, that context is important when considering the politics of any physical practice.

The Energy of Insistence

Although Dunn, Dixon, and McIntyre shared many of Barthes's views regarding corporeality, it is unclear how one should view their improvisations, especially now, decades after their live presentation. What demands did these ensembles make of their audience? How did their work negotiate the limitations of genre? How did expectations of the time (regarding the ways in which men and women should behave, interracial partnerships, the power relations between musicians and dancers, and the status of music and dance as expressive forms) affect the ways in which the improvisers used their bodies to produce sound and motion? These are some of the tight places that their improvisations engaged. Both Moten and the early Barthes suggest that one must consider the contexts and historical moments in which these attempts at improvisational ensemble took place. To approach the work in any other way would reduce its complexity and silence its political underpinnings. In addition, one must engage more than one's vision when witnessing these bodies in sound and motion. While there is no guarantee that one will not misunderstand or oversimplify these collaborations, to even approach their improvisations without grossly reducing their corporeal complexity, history, and politics, one must engage what Moten calls an "ensemble of the senses."

Pondering the sounds evoked by Emmett Till's photograph, containing unbearable shrieks and moans, Moten explains, "The content of the music of this photograph . . . is life, is freedom."[116] Given the questions raised in this book's introduction, it is fitting to emphasize the *ongoing* work that this so-called freedom must entail. While this incessant work inspired McIntyre throughout her career, it unfolded with particular poignancy in her 1980 collaboration with Max Roach and Abbey Lincoln. Dancing within their famous *We Insist! The Freedom Now Suite,* McIntyre struggled to move in relation to sounds that both exceed and are bound with the music of Till's photograph: Abbey Lincoln's screaming. If one really looks at *and* listens to the remnants of this performance, one encounters a full-bodied mode of improvisational and necessarily ongoing protest that jostles the gendered, sexualized, and racialized worlds of music and dance. As the song's title suggests, it does so with an energy that is nothing short of insistence.

CHAPTER 3

Bodies on the Line: Contact Improvisation and Techniques of Nonviolent Protest

On the morning of May 4, 1961, a brave and motley group of travelers—seven black males, three white males, and three white females, varying in age and professional standing but all trained in nonviolence—embarked on what they called the "Freedom Ride."[1] Designed by the Congress of Racial Equality (CORE), the bus ride was meant to commemorate and further the organization's 1947 Journey of Reconciliation, a nonviolent test of a Supreme Court decision that banned segregation on buses that traveled across state lines. This time, riders would test the Supreme Court's1960 decision in *Boynton v. Virginia* prohibiting segregation in the waiting rooms and restaurants of bus terminals.[2] Departing from Washington, D.C., the Freedom Ride aimed to arrive in New Orleans on May 17, the seventh anniversary of *Brown v. Board of Education*. Explaining that they were merely exercising rights granted by the Supreme Court but also that they knew the dangers of doing so, the CORE director James Farmer said, "We were prepared for the possibility of death."[3] Building on the momentum of the student sit-ins, many had come to associate the civil rights movement with "putting your body on the line."[4]

Before departing, the thirteen Freedom Riders divided themselves onto two buses. The first week passed without incident. But early on May 11, the riders had their first violent encounter. Having pulled into the Greyhound terminal in Rock Hill, South Carolina, John Lewis, a member of the Student Nonviolent Coordinating Committee (SNCC) and the youngest Freedom Rider, positioned himself as "first tester," making his way toward the whites' waiting room. The atmosphere was predictably tense. Two white youths quickly blocked the entrance, backed by roughly twenty others. Directed toward the colored entrance to the station, Lewis calmly delivered his standard speech: "I have a right to go in here on grounds of the Supreme Court decision in the *Boynton* case."[5] "Shit on that," was the reply of the white youth, punching Lewis in the stomach. Hit hard, Lewis fell to the ground, and Albert Bigelow, a fellow Freedom Rider trained in the tactics of nonviolent protest, quickly positioned himself between Lewis and his surging attackers.[6]

Although Bigelow responded spontaneously, it is important to recognize that his reaction resulted from mental, spiritual, and physical training. Both Bigelow and Lewis had attended workshops in nonviolent direct action, where they prepared themselves for situations of duress. CORE had conducted workshops in nonviolence since the 1940s. In these workshops, participants engaged in spiritual and philosophical discussions, realizing that "Christianity needed to be modified for politics, and Gandhism modified for American culture."[7] James Lawson, who had spent several years in India studying Gandhi's use of nonviolence, conducted workshops during the late 1950s in Nashville, where he prepared students for a range of demonstrations, including marches, picket lines, and sit-ins. According to Taylor Branch, "Lawson and the other new American Gandhians approached their projects with the care of a chemist. Each step was meticulously planned, executed, and evaluated, with an eye toward isolating behavior and control in response."[8] Their preparations for protest constituted a vital type of research.

In this chapter, I will discuss intersections between the physical techniques that the Freedom Riders drew upon and early innovations in contact improvisation, a partnered form of improvised dance spearheaded by Steve Paxton in the mid-1970s. Previously a dancer in the Merce Cunningham Dance Company and an active participant in the Judson Dance Theater, Paxton explored how bodies move when still or when falling, seeking ways to improvise within unfamiliar situations. What emerged was an improvisational mode of dance making, in which partners move in and out of contact with each other. Although postmodern dance and techniques of nonviolent protest emerged out of distinct histories, traditions, and social demands, I hope to reexamine the politics of contact improvisation in the early years of its development by highlighting the subtle ways in which these explorations coincided.

Other scholars have garnered revealing insights by analyzing nonviolent direct action from the perspective of dance studies. In 2003, Susan Foster wrote an article in *Theatre Journal* entitled "Choreographies of Protest." Discussing the lunch counter sit-ins of 1960, the ACT-UP die-ins that occurred two decades later, and the 1999 World Trade Organization protests in Seattle, Foster explains that she does not view these events as dances, "for that would radically decontextualize their motivation and intent."[9] However, she does view these events as a dance scholar, interested in choreography, spectatorship, and signification. She describes the three protests, noting the training that activists underwent and the conscious positioning of their bodies in relation to changing structures of power. Intent on contesting " 'the volcanic view' of protest as purely spontaneous and lacking in form or technique," Foster asks an important question: "How have these bodies been trained, and how has that training mastered, cultivated, or facilitated their impulses?"[10]

Barbara Browning has also considered the choreography of political struggle. In "Choreographing Postcoloniality: Reflections on the Passing of Edward Said," Browning highlights the dangers of referring to figures such as C. L. R. James, Frantz Fanon, and Mahatma Gandhi as *choreographers*. But she nevertheless proceeds, claiming that "righteous political struggle has had and will continue to have choreographic elements, and politicized dance performance will continue to remind us of the legacy of anticolonial struggle."[11] After admitting, somewhat hesitantly, to urging students to consider the "choreographic force" of Gandhi's march on the Dharasana Salt Works, she notes:

> Nonviolent noncooperation requires a technique of the body which in many ways resembles what contemporary choreographers refer to as "release technique"—but in the charged context of civil disobedience, the movement technique has intense political as well as spiritual ramifications. In 1930 the extraordinary bodily control of thousands of anticolonial protesters who resisted violence embodied a technique that would come to be understood as aesthetically "postmodern" but should be read, even today, as postcolonial in its implications and resonances.[12]

In recognizing that techniques of nonviolent protest resemble instances of postmodern "release technique," Browning paves the way for my discussion of contact improvisation. No doubt, contact improvisation was a predominantly white venture, conducted in the safety of gymnasiums, lofts, and dance studios. Moreover, as Browning argues, movement technique in the charged context of civil disobedience has intense political as well as spiritual ramifications not found in the dance studio. Nevertheless, early contact improvisers investigated small units of movement, at times imperceptible to an outside observer, seeking choices and opportunities for agency—ways to improvise—within extreme situations, most notably while in the act of falling. Although much has been written about contact improvisation's democratic ideals, I am interested in the quest for improvisational possibility during the early years of the form's development, when falling seemed dangerous and the idea of "sharing a dance" was not something to be taken for granted.[13] At its core, contact improvisation is a practice of making oneself ready for a range of shifting constraints. When one looks to historical situations such as the Freedom Rides, in which people have "put their bodies on the line," one begins to see the power of a bodily training such as contact improvisation that seeks calm, confident choices even in situations of duress.

Acquiring Technique

As evidenced by the Freedom Rides, activists in organizations such as CORE engaged in philosophical and spiritual discussions about nonviolence as part of their training. They also carefully considered how they moved. Of particular relevance for the field of dance studies, many civil rights protesters explored the strategic value of falling, slack musculature, and stillness. They also recognized the need for improvisation. This becomes particularly clear in *A Manual for Direct Action,* written in 1964 by the civil rights activists Martin Oppenheimer and George Lakey, with a foreword by Bayard Rustin, who organized the 1947 Journey of Reconciliation and the 1963 March on Washington. Having written a guide for people interested in social change, the authors acknowledge that preparation and training are essential for nonviolent direct action. But they also realize that one cannot provide a set of instructions that would "solve all problems for all time."[14] It is hard to generalize, because one can never know in advance what will happen in moments of confrontation. Therefore, out of necessity, civil rights activists trained themselves to become creative improvisers. As one Freedom Rider described an attempt to support the Freedom Rides at a Mississippi jail-in, "It was a heroic effort at organization improvised under the most difficult conditions."[15]

 As a dance scholar, I am particularly interested in *A Manual for Direct Action* because it contains a great deal of physical description. For example, the authors explain that there are two basic options for responding to a physical attack: stand up and try to make eye contact with the attackers, or fall down. They argue that showing one's face and asking calm questions like "Do you know me? What have I done?" often diffuses violent confrontations. But falling was a widely used method of protecting oneself, as well as others under attack. They explain: "It [falling] is intended to protect the most vital parts of the body, through adopting a crouching position with hands over the head and ears, while lying on the ground. If a buddy is undergoing severe attack, and is on the ground, it is often wise to place yourself between the attackers and the victim by means of falling over the victim, face down, approximating the position of a person doing a 'push-up' on the 'up' part, but keeping your face down and tucked into your chest."[16]

Activists also explored the strategic use of slack musculature and stillness. According to Oppenheimer and Lakey, protestors have the right to demand certain kinds of information from their leaders, including a clear sense of the demonstration's purpose, a plan for concluding the action, and whether or not arrest will be likely. Interestingly, the authors also note that protesters have the right to know "the pros and cons of going limp."[17] In a footnote, the authors explain: "'Going limp' is just what the phrase implies. It is a relaxation of all of the body in a kind of physical non-cooperation with the situation, so that the non-cooperator has to be dragged or carried to wherever authorities want him moved."[18] A few pages later, when discussing possibilities for agitation within a jail, the writers explain that one method is to sit down when outside of a cell or while being moved from one place to another. They state, "An important precaution here is that you should relax your body as much as possible, for tissue can be damaged and torn when you are lifted or dragged if your muscles are tensed."[19]

Although both falling and "going limp" had clear benefits, enabling resistance and diminishing injury, these physical states had social implications that protesters continuously negotiated. For example, demonstrators frequently asked, "Shall we sacrifice our dignified appearance (which has public relations value and maintains a certain personal worth) in order to refuse cooperation with an unjust situation?"[20] Similar questions emerged with the deployment of stillness, also linked with stereotypical images of passivity or compliance that had much to do with gender and race. Susan Foster notes this in her discussion of the student sit-ins, where protestors stood "utterly motionless," requesting to be served at segregated lunch counters. According to Foster, some protesters thought stillness reinforced stereotypes of passivity and therefore abandoned nonviolent methods in favor of more aggressive forms of action; yet, for others, stillness offered a powerful choice in itself.[21]

"Here Are the Facts"

Although few people would consider Ralph Ellison a dance scholar, his novel *Invisible Man* illuminates relations between postmodern bodily practices and techniques of nonviolent protest, illustrating some of the powerful narratives at play as protestors assessed the pros and cons of their movement. One of the most striking scenes in Ellison's novel about race in America, first published in 1947, the same year as CORE's Journey of Reconciliation, involves a degrading display of dancing Sambo marionettes. Relating troubling instances in which spectators are entertained by objects that leap or collapse upon command, the scene encapsulates the most pressing struggles of *Invisible Man,* a novel rife with falling bodies.

"Here are the facts. He was standing and he fell. He fell and he kneeled. He kneeled and he bled. He bled and he died."[22] So *Invisible Man*'s narrator eulogizes the death of Tod Clifton, a dynamic youth leader in Harlem who abandons his activist work late in the novel, only to be killed on the street soon afterward by a white police officer for selling paper Sambo dolls without a permit. When the narrator first encounters Clifton hawking the dolls, he is appalled at the racist kitsch. But his reaction becomes more complex after Clifton's death, when he realizes that the grinning dolls were in fact horrifying marionettes, manipulated by Clifton. Viewing the dolls as "an obscene flouncing of everything human," the narrator examines a paper marionette and exclaims, "The political equivalent of such entertainment is death."[23]

Perhaps the most salient thing to emerge in Ellison's fictional account of marionettes is the desire for autonomous action. Upon discovering fine black thread attached to the paper dolls, the narrator repeatedly asks, "What had made it seem to dance?" Before his death, Clifton had used this same question of causality to taunt and entertain the crowd gathered around him, enthralled by the dancing dolls: "*What makes him happy, What makes him dance, This Sambo, this jambo, this high-stepping joy boy?*"[24] While these questions apply most obviously to the dolls, they also apply to Clifton. The narrator describes Clifton as young, charismatic, and full of potential—a fellow activist in the communist "brotherhood"—and he can't fathom why or how Clifton could have "plunged" into a situation where he performed such degrading acts in public. According to the narrator, something must have made Clifton fall. With great agony, the narrator repeatedly asks who or what could have been responsible. The persistence with which this question appears emphasizes its terrible complexity, bound with a fraught history of racism and the desire for willful mobility as opposed to passivity.

In "Which Way Is Down? Improvisations on Black Mobility," Jason King explains that, historically, black communities in the United States have linked verticality with activism and horizontality with apathy. According to King, these associations are grounded in narratives of racial uplift and the metaphorical "ladder," symbolizing the social mobility in American life made possible by personal will. King traces the rhetoric of uplift from its initial popularization by Booker T. Washington in the late nineteenth century through the black pride movement. Under this view, "Racial progress demands . . . secure footing, resistance against the pull of gravity."[25] King shows the prominence of uplift philosophy's metaphors, citing their appearance in the words of a range of figures, from Malcolm X to Bob Marley, all of whom urge their listeners to "stand up."

Interestingly, the end of King's essay complicates matters, as he notes the exhaustion that frequently accompanies the demands of uplift. According to King, "Uplift requires labor, but in time, exhaustion sets in. Following the display of too much pride, one supposedly falls. But must the fall, downward mobility, inevitably result in shame?"[26] Answering this question, King notes hip-hop, black punk, and the "down low phenomenon" of the late 1990s, a term for hip-hop-identified men who have secret gay sex rather than adhering to the basic tenets of the pride movement, prizing visibility. The bus protests symbolized by Rosa Parks, along with the sit-ins of the 1960s and the workshops that informed actions like the Freedom Rides, were all part of this experimentation. All of these instances recuperate "falling" as having value in political struggle. King explains: "No dead-end is really an end. One can find pride crouching low to the ground, moving under the radar, not just up high, in the air."[27] A few pages later, King proclaims: "Black performance moves toward the co-presence of mobility and immobility, control and freedom. . . . Blackness is ambivalent direction, finding the fall in the ascent, and the ascent in the fall. This is survival."[28]

Both Ellison and King illustrate a sliver of the history, material conditions, and powerful narratives that warn against aestheticizing passivity, often accomplished via limp images of falling or still bodies. However, as seen here, King concludes his essay by issuing a challenge to absolute notions of falling and stillness. King suggests that one can find pride, and perhaps a kind of power, in the act of falling. He also suggests that willful mobility can exist within stillness. This is where techniques of nonviolent protest intersect with postmodern dance techniques, even though each emerged out of distinct traditions with specific social and political demands. Although the overwhelming majority of dancers involved in the early years of contact improvisation were white, and likely more socially "free to fall" than people of color in 1970s America, they too were ambivalent about their relationship with gravity, interested in exploring what King called "the co-presence of mobility and immobility," along with the many falls that exist within any vertical stance.[29]

Learning to Fall

In *The Book of Exultation,* written in 1925, the dance critic A. K. Volinsky discusses verticality as a fundamental principle of classical ballet. To explain why ballerinas dance on their toes, and to make a case for why "everything in ballet is straight, upright, as a taut string that sounds a high note," Volinsky argues that people's impressions vary, depending on whether they see something horizontal or vertical.[30] He states, "In the first case [the horizontal], the psychic sensation is restful and regular, without strong emotion; in the other [the vertical], his soul is made to feel exalted."[31] Volinsky refers to churches, obelisks, columns, and mountains, all as drawing the soul upward. He even uses the evolutionary claim that man moved from living horizontally to standing vertically, a process Volinsky calls the "greatest bloodless revolution in the history of mankind."[32] He concludes by claiming, "Only in ballet do we possess all aspects of the vertical in its exact mathematically formed, universally perceptible expression."[33]

A. K. Volinsky is not alone in his fascination with ballet's virtuosic engagement with gravity. Although ballet's lightness actually is achieved by rotational downward motion, classical ballet has prized verticality, as did most people writing about Western concert dance before the 1970s. In "Classic Ballet: Aria of the Aerial," Lincoln Kirstein explains that ballet "accentuates the area of air," using legwork in an attempt to deny gravity.[34] The end goal, of course, is flight. Ballet's upward striving reaches its pinnacle in the air, exemplified repeatedly in dance history books by Nijinsky's leap.

In contrast, modern dancers such as Isadora Duncan and Doris Humphrey were curious about the ground as much as the air. Doris Humphrey even founded her technique upon the principles of falling and recovering. According to her writings, as well as commentary by John Martin,

Humphrey set out to discover the body's structural proclivities as distinct from emotional reactions. She found that falling constitutes one of the body's primary movements. Humphrey explains: "If you stand perfectly still and do not try to control the movement, you will find that you will begin to fall in one direction. You will fall forward or, probably backward, because you have less to hold you up. This seemed to be a very simple discovery, and yet a tremendously important one, if you're going to start a new technique based on body movement."[35] Friedrich Nietzsche profoundly influenced Humphrey, especially with his discussion of the conflict between Apollonian and Dionysian impulses in man. The tension between a desire for stability and the ecstasy of licentiousness and abandon captivated Humphrey.[36] This tension appeared in Humphrey's dance of fall and recovery, with the Apollonian dance of balance and equilibrium matched with the Dionysian fall. In Humphrey's "My Approach to the Modern Dance" she explains:

> Falling and recovering is the very stuff of movement, the constant flux which is going on in every living body, in all its tiniest parts, all the time. Nor is this all, for the process has a psychological meaning as well. I recognized these emotional overtones very early and instinctively responded very strongly to the exciting danger of the fall, and the repose and peace of recovery.[37]

The oscillation between falling and recovering is evident throughout Humphrey's choreography, most strikingly in dances such as *Two Ecstatic Themes* (1931), in which Humphrey performs a dance of two parts—the first a slow, circular descent to the ground; the second an angular ascent to standing, ending with arms stretched upward to the sky, reminiscent of Volinsky's upward striving. While Humphrey was curious about the risks involved in the act of falling, discourse surrounding her technique generally discusses the fall as yielding or submission, while describing recovery as an act of mastery. When observing Humphrey's choreography, or when learning the technique, one does in fact experience exhilaration in the fall. However, the yielding is always partial. The arms swing, or the torso falls, but there is always the stability of the legs to counterbalance the fall. Or when the legs swing, the torso pulls in opposition. One's entire body never enters a state of free fall, which is where real danger emerges.

As Susan Manning points out, numerous black choreographers—Helmsley Winfield, Edna Guy, and Asadata Dafora in the 1930s, and Katherine

Dunham and Pearl Primus in the 1940s and 1950s—were active at the same time as Doris Humphrey and the other canonized "founders" of modern dance. When one examines this body of work, especially dances by Dafora (born in Sierra Leone and known for his skillful combinations of African and European performance traditions) and Dunham (an African American choreographer and anthropologist who conducted fieldwork in Cuba, Jamaica, Martinique, Trinidad, and Haiti), it becomes clear that modern dance's rejection of ballet's relation to gravity drew from many sources. Brenda Dixon Gottschild makes this argument in *Digging the Africanist Presence in American Performance*. As for modern dancers' relation to gravity and falling, Gottschild argues that "the barefoot dancers reifying contact with the earth, touching it, rolling or lying on it, giving in to it," have African origins.[38] She explains: "These particular components of the New Dance had no coordinates in European concert or folk dance traditions. Those traits live in African and African American dance forms, and modern and postmodern dance received this wisdom from Africanist-inspired American vernacular and pop culture."[39]

In actuality, modern dance's emphasis on the ground incorporates a variety of forms, not all of them directly from Africa. For example, classic modern dances such as José Limón's *Danzas Mexicanas* (1939) and *La Malinche* (1949), in which dancers stomp the ground rhythmically, derive from Limón's childhood in Mexico and his impressions of Spanish bullfights. Movement forms travel in circuitous routes, often changing as they go. Still, one can detect an Africanist presence in the weightedness of modern dance. More ambivalent about the degree to which Western choreographers intentionally appropriated Africanist elements in their work, Susan Manning and John Perpener illustrate the many interactions between midcentury black and white choreographers: Edna Guy studied with Ruth St. Denis, Charles Williams studied with Doris Humphrey and Hanya Holm, and Pearl Primus studied at the New Dance Group.

Still, none of the modernist choreography that emerged from these interactions embraced falling or stillness in the radical sense noted by Jason King. For black choreographers working in the realm of midcentury concert dance, metaphors of uplift were still at play as they tried to get their work presented and recognized by the press. And these metaphors became especially prominent in the work of Alvin Ailey, an African American choreographer who emerged and achieved wide popularity in the late 1950s and early 1960s. Even at the dawn of "postmodern dance," Ailey employed many tenets of the modern tradition, with falls famously followed by recovery. Ailey joined the Lester Horton Dance Theatre in Los Angeles in 1949 and became the company's choreographer after Horton's unexpected death in 1953. The following year, Ailey left for New York and formed the Alvin Ailey Dance Company in 1958. From the company's inception, Ailey was committed to making social statements that revealed "the beauty and elegance of black people; their love of self."[40]

In 1960, Ailey's company for the first time performed *Revelations*, a signature piece set to a suite of black spirituals that bore a deep personal connection to Ailey's memories of Baptist churches from his childhood in Texas. When thinking about falling in Ailey's work, one piece stands out: *Revelations'* solo, "I Want to Be Ready," originally performed by James Truitte but later danced frequently by Dudley Williams. Although *Revelations'* falls are always followed by recovery, "I Want to Be Ready" suggests the need to be prepared, not just for salvation but also for a range of social and historical constraints. In this austere solo, with everything seemingly at stake, dance emerges as a practice of making oneself ready. Long-limbed and dressed entirely in white, the soloist begins seated in fourth position, hands planted firmly on the floor, gazing upward. A series of stretches and contractions ensues, danced in keeping with the slow cadences of the spiritual, beseeching in deep tones, "I want to be ready / I want to be read y/ Lord, ready to put on my long white robe." Several times, the man in white rises from the floor with arms outstretched, only to find the floor again in a controlled, expressive fall. The dance's final descent ends as the man dramatically reaches his right arm across the floor, head down. "I Want to Be Ready" is the last dance in *Revelations'* middle baptismal section, entitled "Take Me to the Water." The third and final section, "Move, Members, Move," builds to a strong, proud pitch of celebratory dancing by the entire Ailey ensemble. Like those of the other canonical modernists, Ailey's falls were followed by triumphant recovery—in the case of *Revelations*, clad in bright-yellow, Sunday best.

While rebellious in many ways, the fall in modern dance was controlled and seldom lasted for long. Even as dancers involved in the Judson Dance Theater began to challenge the modern dancer's vertical stance and relation to gravity during the 1960s, complete inversions and a willingness to suspend control remained anomalous. As Steve Paxton states when discussing Trisha Brown's *Trillium*, first performed at Maidman Playhouse on March

24, 1962: "It was odd to see a handstand in a dance at that time. It was odd to see people off their feet doing anything but a very controlled fall."[41] In the realm of concert dance, it would take the postmodern dance experiments of the 1970s, most notably contact improvisation, to rigorously investigate falling and dismantle the corresponding opposition between mastery and submission.

Steve Paxton's "Small Dance"

In January 1972, Steve Paxton and a group of eleven male students performed *Magnesium* in an Oberlin College gymnasium. According to Cynthia Novack, people commonly refer to *Magnesium* as the beginning of contact improvisation, the "seminal work."[42] As the men hurl themselves at each other, fall, roll about, and get up again, thunderlike sounds echo throughout the gymnasium. Their arms flail as they collide deliberately and aggressively with one another. After several minutes of this structured, vigorous improvisation, the men rise individually to "The Stand," a signature Paxton exercise also referred to as the "Small Dance." Facing various directions, the men stay motionless for several minutes. While the dancers' vertical stillness contrasts with the previous swirl of motion, one nevertheless can detect a slight swaying motion as the dancers move through and around their vertical axes. Paxton explains, "All you have to do is stand up and relax—you know—and at a certain point you realize that you've relaxed everything that you can relax but you're still standing and in that standing is quite a lot of minute movement."[43] In order to stand, there's a constant background noise, a small dance in the body's effort to remain vertical.

In keeping with Jason King's observations about the copresence of mobility and immobility, Paxton's Stand troubles notions of absolute verticality or bodily stillness. Moreover, as contact improvisation developed as a form, standing was used as a discipline, teaching the dancer that the body works reflexively in a dependable way to protect itself when falling. The goal eventually became to maintain the calmness of the stand even in extreme, adrenalized states of dancing. At one point in *Fall after Newton,* a video tracing the first eleven years of contact improvisation's development, Paxton discusses Nancy Stark Smith's decisions during a risky fall as the image appears in slow motion: "In order to develop this aspect of the form we had to be able to survive it."[44] At this point in the video, Stark Smith cascades from Curt Siddall's shoulder, creating an extended arc downward, only to have her head clear the floor by inches. The video lingers in the moment where her head brushes inches from the floor, presenting smudged traces of her body's arc as she falls slowly toward the ground. Paxton explains: "It is useful to re-train the reflexes to extend the limbs rather than contract them during a fall. During this very disorienting fall, Nancy's arms manage to cradle her back, and this spreads the impact onto a greater area. And she doesn't stop moving."[45]

In this narration, Paxton emphasizes the need for dancers to retrain their reflexes in order to fall safely. But beyond safety—something of obvious concern to activists training in nonviolent direct action—contact improvisers cultivated an awareness of the many physical possibilities that exist even while falling. Paxton explains elsewhere in the video's narration: "Beyond [Isaac] Newton's third law, we discover that for every action several equal and opposite reactions are possible. Therein lies an opportunity for improvisation."[46] According to Paxton, dancers have *several* possibilities in moving through the fall, depending upon momentum, weight distribution between partners, and the overall tone of the improvisation. Although there is no way to tell through video whether dancers react instinctually or by way of conscious design, one nevertheless can trace directional shifts in momentum and discern possible lines of flight or fall in any given moment. This quest for improvisational possibility constitutes a vital skill. Even when dancers appear "still," less muscularly held than their modernist forbears, they are in fact engaged in a "small dance," alert and ready to improvise in a variety of ways.

The Grit of Contact Improvisation

As dancers became adept at the form and more comfortable with falling, both the "risks" and the look of contact improvisation changed. Nancy Stark Smith explains: "Maybe, because you had seen something on tape, or live, you would try it. If it worked consistently, it might become vocabulary."[47] Years of analyzing their experiences and imitating successful moves enabled contact improvisers to codify an aesthetic and figure out the mechanics of a new form. As a result, contact improvisation has changed significantly since the early years of *Magnesium*. The rough and often clunky collisions have turned into fantastic falls as the dancers have learned to listen to their partners and share weight as opposed merely to banging up against it. Smoothness and cooperation between partners became goals. It is not clear, however, that this smoothness signifies untrammeled progress. In a 1984 issue of *Contact Quarterly*, Nancy Stark Smith recognizes and laments the loss of discord seen in the early days:

> I've learned a lot from Contact Improvisation about coordinating with the forces-that-be: Accepting gravity, falling, following momentum, blending with a partner's movements—i.e., "going with the flow." But lately, I've been feeling feisty. . . . I find myself playing against the forces—making myself heavy instead of light when a lift starts, adding a splash to the easy pouring of weight, insisting instead of yielding, adding fierce to gentle, no to yes. It's a start. I've been in the harmony business a long time now.[48]

Over the years, a "grace" has undoubtedly developed in contact improvisation, and Stark Smith seems to have recognized its troubling consequences. It is important, then, to look for moments in contact improvisation where flow gets broken—jarring moments reminiscent of the early *Magnesium* days but also moments of apparent stillness or subtle hiccups of miscommunication. As Kent De Spain describes his experience in improvised decision making, "Sometimes in the hyperawareness of improvisation, there are microseconds of stillness between movements (a feeling I might call 'hovering') where I sense an actual muscular tension that feels like my body wants to go in several directions."[49] These breaks in flow constitute the often ignored, but crucial, grit of contact improvisation. They serve as visible reminders, for those not actually dancing, that negotiations are taking place, even when the fall appears smooth and full of grace or when the bodies seem dangerously passive.

Interestingly, Stark Smith's remarks about her newfound feistiness were inspired by a discussion between Steve Paxton and Bill T. Jones, moderated by Mary Overlie on December 4, 1983. This heated debate constitutes a significant "break in flow," interrupting narratives about contact improvisation and postmodern dance to insist upon the importance of difference, as well as social and historical context, when considering the political potential of any physical practice. According to Stark Smith, "Several times during the talk [between Jones and Paxton], I felt myself wincing at the action as one might while watching a boxing match when the swing connects."[50] The discussion, which took place after both dancers performed solos, quickly became edgy as Jones said, "I think that there is a *thing* which is that there are people who are *Contact* people. Is this true?"[51] Of course, the presumption was that Paxton *was* and Jones *was not* a "contact person."

Throughout the conversation, Jones appeared alienated, angry, and at times insecure. He admits that, on the way to the talk, his partner, Arnie Zane, had urged him not to "let this get polarized, because you [and Steve] probably have a lot more in common than you do *not* in common."[52] But the conversation was polarized. Although the two choreographers occasionally found common ground, the tension between them increased throughout the talk. Jones was concerned that Paxton, and the audience, didn't like his dancing—that they didn't "believe" in what he was doing on stage. In retaliation, Jones claimed that Paxton's inquiry into vibrations and small units of movement was ungenerous. Jones explains: "The only problem I ever had is that I thought that it might be ungenerous. . . . Your experimentation . . . in a way. . . . I'd like to see more movement. Not necessarily just more, but more about dancing more about the history."[53]

Each artist made several compelling points. They are both phenomenal dancers, dedicated to thinking about dance. But the two talked past each other, hashing out their respective relationships to dance history and to a particular "tradition." At the time of their conversation, Jones wanted to do big movements in big houses, while Paxton wanted to create a research branch of dance. Arguing that several choreographers already perform large-scale works aimed at entertainment, Paxton asked, "Is it ungenerous to decide that maybe there's a glut of that material on the market?"[54]

Paxton made a valid point, but Jones didn't seem to hear it. Arguing that it was no longer 1963, Jones lambasted "avant-garde" artists who reject tradition, claiming: "I feel like, for me, a lot of people making this type of work, they're babies. They really are babies. And they will never grow because they have prejudices, so many prejudices."[55] As a gay, black choreographer, committed in the 1980s to identity-based work, Jones described both the Judson Dance Theater and the Grand Union as "a bunch of precocious children that were being encouraged to play."[56] When Paxton, who was involved in both projects, objected that the Grand Union and the Judson Dance Theater were different endeavors that occurred in different decades, Jones responded: "Oh boy, here we go. Well, to me they're all alike."[57]

The tension between Paxton and Jones is palpable even in the written transcript of their conversation. One of the most interesting moments emerged when Paxton failed to recognize that a spoken solo performed by

Jones had been largely improvised. Jones explained that he likes to "quote" shapes from recognizable traditions such as ballet and "ethnic dance," using his feelings and the surrounding space to hold these eclectic pieces together. Doubting that the concept of "quoting" could be applied to an embodied act, Paxton proceeded to describe how his interest in minuscule vibration differed from Jones's interest in larger, recognizable chunks of movement. Here is where the misrecognition occurred. Paxton pronounced, "You're working on that kind of literary level where the quotes are instantly known and you're playing with, it seems to me, dance movement rather in the way you played with the poem that you read."[58] Jones then interrupted Paxton by stating sharply, "No, I wasn't reading it, I was improvising it." Paxton responded, "Really. Well anyway . . ."[59]

Although the conversation's momentum quickly swept away Paxton's dismissive flash of misrecognition, his oversight raises significant questions about improvisation's role in postmodern dance, questions that became intensely pronounced with the emergence of contact improvisation: What does improvised dance look like? And whose tradition is it? These questions echo the tensions that existed as Judith Dunn and Bill Dixon began to work together, each emerging out of distinct traditions, with different approaches to improvisation and beliefs about its political significance. Of course, to even suggest that improvisation *looks* a certain way is to obscure its power as a process rather than a product, hardened and made legible by distinctive aesthetic characteristics.

At a superficial level, the distinction between "contact people" and "non-contact people" refers to the different trajectories of Jones's and Paxton's careers. In a more complicated sense, however, the notion that some people are "contact people" while others are not demands that one consider bodies and their historical circumstances. Jones clearly suggests that contact improvisation was more exclusionary than its practitioners liked to admit. Even within the safety of dance studios, surrounded by contact improvisation's egalitarian rhetoric, imbalances of power abound. It is easier for some to move in particular ways than others, depending on the context, and the stakes are not always the same. Stark Smith's desire to say "no" more often, using her body to obstruct rather than facilitate flow, suggests a desire to complicate gendered compliance. Somewhat similarly, as seen in Ellison and King, historical racism and powerful narratives of uplift complicate the implications of falling and stillness.

In *Sharing the Dance: Contact Improvisation and American Culture,*
Cynthia Novack notes that contact improvisers, especially in the 1970s,
viewed the form as an egalitarian communal activity. Recently, Ann Cooper
Albright joined Novack in lauding contact improvisation's political possibilities. In "Open Bodies: (X)Changes of Identity in Capoeira and Contact Improvisation," Albright argues that contact improvisation offers an improved
way of "being-with-others in the world," where dancers learn that "changes
and exchanges of identity [are] possible without sacrificing one's own experience of groundedness."[60] According to Albright, these "(X)Changes" arise
out of the form's emphasis on spontaneity and play; its privileging of disorientation and fluidity; and its willingness to confront "others" in a complex,
bodily way, where boundaries begin to blur.[61] Albright maintains that one
can retrain and retheorize bodies.

A profound hope for a better world drives Albright's project. Still, her
work raises many questions. Surely, dancers can mediate various learned
techniques. But can a dancer "retrain" his or her position amid racism and
sexism? Moreover, I wonder about the extent to which a meaningful "exchange of identity" can occur within contact improvisation, especially if it re-
presses or doesn't acknowledge the sexual, gendered, raced body. I also
worry about romanticizing disorientation in a social landscape that is always
already unsteady in its shifting power relations. There are times when disorientation can be a burden, if not outright debilitating.

As seen in the exchange between Paxton and Jones, contact improvisation did not offer a way to *transcend* difference or fraught social encounters.
Power relations did not evaporate as people began to share a dance. Nevertheless, as I've argued throughout this chapter, contact improvisation, especially as a practice during its early years, did widen the possibilities for improvising within tense situations—provided one could hold onto the
importance of "grit" and remember that sometimes one must use one's body
as an obstruction rather than go with the flow. A graceful dance does not necessarily indicate progress or harmony, and the blurring of boundaries, even if
possible, is not necessarily a good thing.

In closing, I do not wish to suggest that contact improvisation is protest
in the sense that the Freedom Rides were. Nor do I mean to suggest that in
situations of violent confrontation, one should start dancing like Nancy
Stark Smith. Still, it is also possible to see how contact improvisation's quest
for improvisational possibility even in the midst of falling might be mobilized

in other contexts. At its core, contact improvisation is a practice of making oneself ready for a range of ever-shifting surprises and constraints. When one looks to historical situations in which people have strategically "put their bodies on the line," one begins to see the power of a bodily training such as contact improvisation that seeks choices and opportunities for agency—the calmness that gets practiced in the Stand—even in unfamiliar situations of physical duress.

CHAPTER 4 The Breathing Show: *Improvisation*
in the Work of Bill T. Jones

During the late 1990s, critics, fans, and even Bill T. Jones
himself began talking about the artist's move from explicitly political, identity-based works to an investigation of aesthetics and pure movement.[1] They
talked about the more conventional makeup of Jones's ensemble, particularly
the fact that Lawrence Goldhuber and Alexandra Beller, dancers whom the
New York Times described as "imperfect" because "chubbier than the
norm," were no longer in the company.[2] They discussed the fact that Jones
rarely used text and was no longer confrontational. He danced to Beethoven
and performed at Lincoln Center with the Chamber Music Society. In a 1997
interview with Richard Covington, Jones explained this shift in his work by
stating: "It's not quite as sexy to talk about. What was being said in those
earlier works was as important as how it was being danced. Here, I'm trying
to think about how it's danced first, trusting that the political, social, all
those things are in our bodies literally, and in the eyes of the beholder."[3]

This chapter traces the trajectory of Jones's career, from his rejection of
contact improvisation, to his aggressive, politically charged works of the
1980s, to his controversial return to form. I discuss the role of improvisation
across these shifts, paying particular attention to *The Breathing Show*, an unprecedented evening of solo performance by Jones, made in the twilight of his
performing career. Jones began to work on *The Breathing Show* in 1998,
when, at the age of forty-six, he found himself both embroiled in controversy
surrounding his renewed interest in form and concerned about his legacy.
The more he worked on the evening-length performance, the more important
improvisation became, whether in the form of his banter with the audience
or in his improvised talking solo *Floating the Tongue*. According to Jones,
"It's curious and unsettling, but I feel *The Breathing Show* only began to
come alive when I decided to speak and to allow myself to improvise."[4]

I discuss how improvisation "enlivened" *The Breathing Show* by analyzing the relationship between Jones's onstage presence and *Ghostcatching*, an
installation that used motion-capture technology to present traces of Jones's
prior improvisations. With *Ghostcatching*, Jones's improvisations became
virtual, moving in a sense *beyond* the body. How then, if at all, does the work
hold onto its social concerns and critical perspective on issues of identity?
Does *Ghostcatching* represent Jones's most radical formalist turn? Can politics transpire in a virtual dance that allows neither sweat nor skin, primary
markers of labor and race, to appear on stage? For Jones, these questions are
bound with the issue of whether freedom consists in the ability to follow or
to deviate from formal conventions—to affirm pure form or critique it. In
more general terms: is pure form escape or constraint? And likewise with improvisation, as practiced in certain established avant-garde contexts: does it
represent freedom or its absence? Jones suggests that both possibilities involve degrees of constraint and conformism, and *The Breathing Show* reflects
on this tension explicitly. In this respect, Jones's point is perfectly in keeping
with this book's broader critique of freedom as something that can be
achieved or that consists in anything other than the struggle to realize it.
Freedom, Jones seems to imply, consists in the perpetual readiness demanded
by a critical stance toward oneself and the world in general.

Insisting on the Personal

As Jones prepared for a career as a professional dancer during the early
1970s, he worked diligently to acquire what he thought was foundational
technique. He spent difficult hours in ballet classes, trying to emulate the
clear articulation of highly trained bodies and mold his body into classical
lines. It was a frustrating experience. Jones explains: "The mental and physical tortures of the dance studio offered no connection to any sense of lyric
flight. . . . The ballet barre became the site of a battle between what I was and
what I willed myself to be."[5] ⬚ ones a re-
prieve from this grueling attem⬚ g to Jones,
in hidden moments during his⬚ he improvised alone in the studio, which⬚ ep truth of
movement."[6]

In addition to hidden mom⬚ mprovisa-
tion offered Jones another alte⬚ h his conversations with Steve Paxton d⬚ vise, Jones

was exhilarated by his first encounter with contact improvisation. It was the summer of 1973—a heady time for Jones, when life as a dancer seemed difficult but full of possibility. Having recently transferred from SUNY-Binghamton to SUNY-Brockport, Jones picked up a flyer on campus: "IF YOU LIKE TO ROCK AND ROLL OR LINDY HOP, DO AIKIDO, OR MAKE LOVE—COME ON DOWN AND JOIN US AT THE CONTACT IMPROVISATION WORKSHOP WITH LOIS WELK."[7] Jones was acquainted with Welk and had already begun to study improvisation with Richard Bull. According to Jones, "It was in an improvisation class taught by Richard Bull that I discovered that dance wasn't only about pointing my feet or making lines in space. It was about how I could solve problems."[8] So Jones convinced his partner, a white Jewish man named Arnie Zane, to attend the contact improvisation workshop with him. They were enlivened by the experience. As a sign of the times, Zane described his initial foray into contact improvisation as "better than tripping."[9]

In Welk's workshops, dancers learned the basic principles of contact improvisation: how to dance in physical contact with others, how to "share weight," and how to fall. According to Jones, "Suddenly, dancing was not only about trying to fly. Dancing was about listening, making sense out of an intensely personal exchange as private as lovemaking."[10] Jones explains that he was ready for an increased awareness of touch and everyday movement. Reminiscing about his initial exposure to contact improvisation, he explains: "Here I found the delicacy of two foreheads together, the contact point sliding across the eye sockets and down to the chin. Two throats then touching at a single point, then clavicles and shoulders, sternums and bellies. . . . Physical awareness was richer than ever before."[11]

Improvisation continued to be important for Jones, even as he became technically proficient and well-known as a choreographer. Returning to Binghamton after a brief excursion to San Francisco in the early 1970s, Jones, Zane, and Welk joined the dancer Jill Becker and the poet Ira Bruckner and moved into a wreck of a building, where they made work under the auspices of the American Dance Asylum. During this time, Jones choreographed several pieces: *Entrances* (1974), *Track Dance* (1974), and *Everybody Works/All Beasts Count* (1975), which garnered Jones's first grant as well as positive recognition from the *New York Times*. But despite his increasing success as a choreographer, Jones felt very much alone. Although the Dance Asylum was an exercise in countercultural communal living, it was not a substitute for

Jones's family. Jones explains: "Dance Asylum was a federation of artists, not a family. . . . A kind of heaviness would overtake me at times. I'd put on Mahalia Jackson, improvise in the studio, and find myself crying."[12] While improvisation initially offered Jones a reprieve from the demands of technical training, before long, it also offered Jones a way to connect to a sense of personal history, an emotional connection that fueled much of his later politicized work.

   Floating the Tongue was precisely this type of dance. The piece was originally created in 1978, and its title refers to a Buddhist meditation practice where one concentrates on the "simple" task of floating one's tongue within one's mouth. Jones created *Floating the Tongue* for a recital at New York's Kent School for Boys. Wanting to dispel the notion that dancers don't think while dancing, Jones created a challenging, four-part improvisation. To begin, Jones improvises until he arrives at a movement phrase that is set in his memory and repeatable. In a recent performance, Jones created a stationary sequence wherein a series of undulations ripples through isolated parts of his body: his head, his right shoulder, and then his hips. Jones then punctuates this sequential movement with clear lines and recognizable shapes. At one point, his arms form a wide T, extending out from his shoulders to the farthest reaches of the stage. A bit later, Jones slowly rises into a delicate relevé. The phrase ends as Jones extends his arms on a front diagonal. With eyes closed, he first brings his palms to his face and then brushes them slowly down the front of his body.

   For the second iteration of the phrase, Jones describes each movement in as much detail as possible while dancing: "Slowly allow face to slide forward . . . right shoulder rolls forward, North position, and retrograde to the back . . . center the weight . . . and the ass reaches to the back . . . as the heels drop down to fifth position, arms extend in second."[13] Although one immediately sees the challenge of speaking while dancing, one also sees the abundance of movement at any moment during the phrase—far more than one can describe.

   During the third iteration of the phrase, Jones continues to talk, but with minimal self-censorship or self-consciousness. He dances the sequence while continuously saying what he thinks and feels. Here, one begins to see the "emotional meaning" that lives in gestures of the body. As his physical undulations unfold, Jones exclaims: "Always saying something degrading about blacks like step and fetch it, like long-necked nigger. Why do I say that

. . . and front and back and front and back . . . Always . . . Trisha and the way she swings her hips . . . What does it mean to be an adult? To own property? . . . Open me up, oh lord, open my heart . . . I'm sweating."[14] As Barbara Browning explains, "The meanings of that embodied text are inevitably personal and political, difficult, and engaged with the world. "[15]

According to the score, the final iteration can develop in any direction, with Jones's conscious mind leading or following. According to Jones, "It [the final phase of the improvisation] has to have the contours like a good jazz riff. Even when you lose the melody, you can still feel it."[16] The dancer also has the option to stop moving entirely. As a result, this final sequence varies tremendously in timing and volume, with remarkable expressive range. Jones whispers and screams, repeats movements, and occasionally stands still. Guttural sounds frequently emerge, interrupted by recognizable words and phrases. With far looser strictures than the previous iterations, the task recedes, becoming less apparent than the actual dance that unfolds. As Jones performs *Floating the Tongue,* his improvisational skill emerges, as does his bold willingness to be publicly vulnerable. One never knows what will come out.

Floating the Tongue did far more than reveal the fact that dancers think. In his memoir, *Last Night on Earth,* Jones explains that the creation of *Floating the Tongue* drew upon memories of his mother. According to Jones, "My mother's praying was the first theater I ever saw—and the truest. "[17] *Floating the Tongue* allows Jones to enter a similar state of being, where he accesses layers of history as well as deep levels of meaning that exist within movement. Discussing a particularly moving performance in February 2000, Browning notes that Welk's presence in the audience provoked in Jones a host of associations and memories, most notably the death of Arnie Zane, who died of AIDS in 1988. Browning explains: "It [Zane's passing] tumbled out of Jones's mouth in painful fragments, amid a rush of other images and associations—some politically overdetermined, some excruciatingly personal. One had the sense of being witness to an extraordinary moment, in which poignant personal memories and political history were inextricably intertwined."[18]

Like much of Jones's later work, *Floating the Tongue* made some people uncomfortable. For example, Arlene Croce, the *New Yorker*'s longtime dance critic and one of Jones's most famous detractors, dismissively wrote that Jones had worked himself into a tizzy with *Floating the Tongue.* Jones explains: "I was hurt by this. And offended. This 'tizzy' is something I have claimed as an inheritance. Perhaps in her experience it did not seem genuine, or perhaps it seemed too genuine—embarrassing, even—but for me it is an internal part of the strategy that allows me to make art."[19]

By introducing autobiography and emotional experience into his work via spoken improvisation, Jones ushered an important challenge to 1970s postmodern dance. As noted earlier, Jones believed in the utopian project of contact improvisation when he was a student during the early 1970s. According to Jones, contact improvisation "encouraged an unselfconscious, direct physical intimacy in which all differences—weight, size, psychological temperament, even gender and race—were negated in favor of cohesion—tissue to tissue, bone to bone, muscle to muscle."[20] But by 1983, as noted in the previous chapter, Jones no longer felt like a "contact person."[21]

This switch grew out of Jones's work with Arnie Zane. As the two men choreographed and performed together during the late 1970s and early 1980s, a productive tension arose between Zane's reluctance to include autobiographical material in their dances and Jones's desire to do so. Despite a great deal of criticism, Jones increasingly provided a place for the personal in his work. In retrospect, he explains: "We had to respond to the fact that I was a black man who used the word 'nigger' in the context of a work that had been a moment ago—we thought—purely about form, time, repetition, maybe the personalities of the dancers." Angry at repeatedly being reduced to a "black choreographer," Jones began to challenge notions of formal purity by exploring the politics of identity.

Alienated from the white avant-garde dance scene, Jones became inspired during the late 1970s and early 1980s by the artist Vito Acconci, who strove to aggravate his audience, whether by banging against pipes when people were in earshot or masturbating in art galleries. Jones employed a different strategy: he used improvised movement and language to challenge the racist assumptions of his audience and the New York dance world.[22] Knowing that his dancing body often appeared beautiful and seductive, Jones quickly realized that language could complicate matters in useful ways. According to Jones, by the early 1980s, he was no longer preoccupied with pleasing his audience: "With the Acconci strategy in place, I was able to deconstruct this identity. Deconstruction yielded solos that were confessional, often painful, taking unpleasant emotions and exposing them spontaneously in a fashion that was brutal on both the audience and me."[23]

In 1981, the American Dance Festival invited Jones to perform as part of its "Emerging Generations Program" in Durham, North Carolina. Jones performed an improvised solo based on a series of oppositional statements. He pronounced to the audience, "I love women." Then, "I hate women. I love white people. I hate white people. I'd like to kiss you. I'd like to tear your fucking heart out. Why didn't you leave us in Africa? I'm so thankful for the opportunity to be here."[24] In the *New York Times,* Jack Anderson reviewed the program, exclaiming that Jones's four-part *Social Intercourse* was the most "emotionally explosive" work of the evening. He claimed that the finale's tremendous "crescendo of rage made the evening an evocation of the frustration and anxieties of black Americans."[25] The solo shocked many people, and Jones wasn't invited back to the festival for ten years.

The Bill T. Jones/Arnie Zane Dance Company was founded in 1982 and immediately became known for the diversity of its members. Together, Jones and Zane produced a range of works that challenged the avant-garde. During the mid-1980s, they made works like *Fever Swamp, Holzer Duet . . . Truisms,* and *Freedom of Information,* while managing the demands of a well-known company with financial needs and international touring. But Zane became sick and, in 1985, was diagnosed with HIV. Jones also tested positive, but it was Zane who began to commute to New York City for chemotherapy. The couple found themselves amid a far-reaching AIDS epidemic. In his memoir, Jones explains: "Watching Arnie, I felt as though I was standing on the shore of a lake in which he was swimming. He would disappear for long periods of time, then, at completely unpredictable moments, he would come up for air. As the day wore on, he seemed to move farther and farther from shore and to surface less frequently."[26] Although Zane died in 1988, the company continues to be called the Bill T. Jones/Arnie Zane Dance Company.

A Seemingly Formal Turn

Two years after Zane died of AIDS, Jones committed himself to making work that dealt explicitly with his identity. Regarding *Last Supper at Uncle Tom's Cabin/The Promised Land* (1990), Jones states, "I reasoned that if my time was limited, that if I was to follow Arnie soon . . . I would speak in a voice that was decidedly African-American."[27] *Last Supper,* which includes a distillation of Harriet Beecher Stowe's novel and excerpts from Sojourner Truth's *Ain't I a Woman?* and LeRoi Jones's *Dutchman,* enabled Jones to grapple with a series of social and political questions: "Was Uncle Tom a disgrace to his race? A romanticization of servitude? Is this high-minded, propagandistic literary work of any relevance to us today? What happened to the bold notion of liberty that fueled this novel?"[28] The piece ends with a half-hour section called *The Promised Land,* where a diverse cast culled from local communities fills the stage, gently disrobing to create a broad image of humanity. It was Jones's attempt to affirm a commonality that bravely embraced difference.

Between Jones's overtly political *Last Supper* and the discussions about formal purity that encircle his work of the late 1990s, a notorious controversy erupted over his 1994 piece *Still/Here*. For the piece, Jones journeyed around the country conducting movement workshops with terminally ill volunteers. According to Jones, "*Still/Here* I thought was going to be a work that nobody would find controversial—there was no controversy. It wasn't about my black rage. It was going to be unassailably about human experience, or so I thought."[29] The evening-length work that Jones choreographed for his dance company drew elements of its movement vocabulary from these workshops and incorporated sound and video of workshop participants. It was a poetic dance about survival, famously denounced by *New Yorker* critic Arlene Croce as "victim art."

Refusing on principle to see *Still/Here,* Croce proclaimed the piece "undiscussable" for the critic. In a particularly brutal passage, showing galling privilege and narrow vision, Croce explains:

> I can't review someone I feel sorry for or hopeless about. As a dance critic, I've learned to avoid dancers with obvious problems—overweight dancers (not fat dancers; Jackie Gleason was fat and was a good dancer), old dancers, dancers with sickled feet, or dancers with physical deformities who appear nightly in roles requiring beauty of line. In quite another category of undiscussability are those dancers I'm *forced* to feel sorry for because of the way they present themselves: as dissed blacks, abused women, or disfranchised homosexuals—as performers, in short, who make out of victimhood victim art.[30]

The *New Yorker* article incensed Jones and continues to weigh heavily on the production and reception of his work. To this day, he solemnly refuses to mention Croce by name. But Croce was not a lone "guardian" during the culture wars and identity politics of the 1990s. Jones and his company frequently encountered protests and pickets in their tours around the country. After a while, Jones explains, "I had sort of had it. . . . This is not what I want to do. And so I began to think about leaving art or going more deeply into what I loved to begin with, which was movement."[31] By the late 1990s, Jones seemed to have traveled full circle with his renewed interest in form. The return, however, was not so simple.

One could argue that Jones's formal turn was overdetermined by a particular political moment that might eventually disappear, if it hasn't already. But this line of argument in no way loosens the bond between politics and form, shifting across cultures and historical periods but never disappearing. Jones's renewed interest in the "how" of dancing differs from a naive retreat into a land of imagined formal purity. Jones explains quite clearly: "I think it's impossible to perform any ritualized activity in a public sphere that is politically neutral. I think it's impossible. All art forms, including Merce Cunningham, who is my favorite choreographer, Merce claims that it's politically neutral, it's not. Trisha [Brown], who is a great teacher to me, who I love, thinks it's politically neutral, it's not."[32] As a black man dancing in a time and place where whiteness is largely invisible and so-called formal purity looks suspiciously like traditionally white aesthetics, Jones understands the naïveté, the exclusivity of imagining a formal realm free of politics.

In a recent interview at New York University, Jones asked an auditorium full of students, "Are we there yet?" Nudging the auditorium full of white students to realize the distance we have yet to travel in pursuit of such looking, Jones continues, "Why can't *I* be free?" Committed to blackness in all its variance and doubtful of our collective "there-ness" with respect to race-free looking, Jones nevertheless maintains his renewed interest in form. Pushing boundaries and asking questions even when the answers are unclear, Jones urges the students: "Can you see with two sets of eyes? Can you see the identity, and also see the form? What is at stake on that stage?" Recognizing that Jones's talk about pure movement never strays from an awareness of the stakes involved, one gets the sense that he doesn't want to retreat from the political. He just does not want to foreground it constantly, using the same vocabulary that he used in the 1980s and early 1990s. Caught in this bind, Jones calls for a complicated doubling: "Can you see with two sets of eyes?"[33]

The most radical aspect of Jones's call, and perhaps the easiest to miss, is that he genuinely seeks a sum larger than its parts. He rejects an either/or situation, where the viewer alternates between focusing on identity one moment and form the next. Either strand of Jones's vision, no matter how celebratory the discourse, is problematic in isolation. He asks: "When you look at my stage now, can you look with two sets of eyes? Do you see the sexual preference of the person, the race of the person, the gender of the person, and then, can you see what they're doing? And how the two come together to create a vision that is, that makes you want to look more carefully, want to dance, to want to touch one another."[34] In seeking an "ethics of transcultural performance," the dance scholar André Lepecki configures a similar choreographic task for the viewing audience. Claiming "laziness in seeing" as dance viewers' primary pathology when faced with a body from another culture, Lepecki calls for a delicate partnering between audience and dancer: "How can my audience body become a partner to those bodies dancing for me?"[35] Rather than brutally attempting to wipe out difference with an imagined formal purity, or remaining content in a distanced relationship of "respect" while reducing the other to his or her most obvious markers of alterity, Jones urges audiences to meet the performer as a partner. The difficulty, of course, as discussed earlier in relation to Roland Barthes, is to realize one's pursuit of pleasure without overwhelming the other.

Ghostcatching's *Cool Blue Lurchings*

In 1998 and 1999, the digital media artists Paul Kaiser and Shelley Eshkar worked with Merce Cunningham to produce *Hand-drawn Spaces* and *Biped,* motion-capture pieces that met with critical acclaim. With motion capture, reflective sensors are placed on a moving body. Cameras surrounding the dancer then record the movements of each sensor in time and space, feeding this data into a computer for animators, in this case Kaiser and Eshkar, to choreograph and design. Cunningham, long interested in the type of formalism that Jones challenged throughout his career, didn't care whether Kaiser and Eshkar's technology captured his dancers' "identities." For example, in *Biped,* Cunningham taught movement sequences to two dancers, one male and one female. Their motion was then captured and drawn without sexual markings, enabling the combination of their phrases. In a sense, the dancers were merged. But if Cunningham attracted Kaiser and Eshkar with his abstract, linear movement, his focus on form and his willingness to experiment with technology, most famously with Life-Forms software, Bill T. Jones attracted the digital artists for different reasons. According to Kaiser, they were intrigued by Jones's movement style, which they saw as more fluid and less angular than Cunningham's and thus more challenging to capture with their new technology. The other reason, however, had to do with Jones as an outspoken, politicized, gay, black choreographer. Kaiser explains, "We were also interested in working with Bill, not as a choreographer of a group, but as a choreographer of himself: of his own body, of his own identity."[36]

Presented with the opportunity to collaborate with accomplished digital media artists and motion-capture technology, Jones was eager to experiment, but not without reservations. Intrigued and impressed with Kaiser and Eshkar's previous work with Cunningham, but forthright in his concerns regarding the project, Jones clearly told his collaborators, "I do not want to be a disembodied, denatured, de-gendered series of lines moving in a void."[37] According to Kaiser, whereas Cunningham's *Hand-drawn Spaces* "reveled in the supposed freedom of abstracted motion, *Ghostcatching* would question it."[38]

After *Ghostcatching* premiered at the Cooper Union in January 1999, Jones, Kaiser, and Eshkar returned to the motion-capture studio to rework parts of the piece. A video version then appeared within Jones's tour of *The Breathing Show*.

As Ghostcatching *begins, blue light appears on stage, projected onto a giant screen. A hand-drawn outline of a rectangular box then emerges, followed by a sketchlike figure, the motion-captured Jones inside the box. The figure moves through a series of six positions, lettered A through F, while a voice calls out the letter with each shift of position. The figure, clearly male, clearly Jones, sculpts himself into linear movements—sharp lines—much like profiled figures within an Egyptian frieze.*

Before long, another Jones emerges and moves through the boundaries of the box to dance briefly around its borders before disappearing. While the figure on the inside continues to move through his sequence of lettered movements, a series of bodies appears, each one more fully drawn. They dance fluidly, occupying expanses of space outside of the box, leaving traces with their hands and feet. Much like the famous photographs of Picasso, lights seemingly attach to the figures' distal ends, enabling them to draw with their dancing. A leg gracefully arcs into arabesque, leaving a semi-circle of light in its wake. Another figure falls into a squat with arms raised, once again marking the pathways of his body.

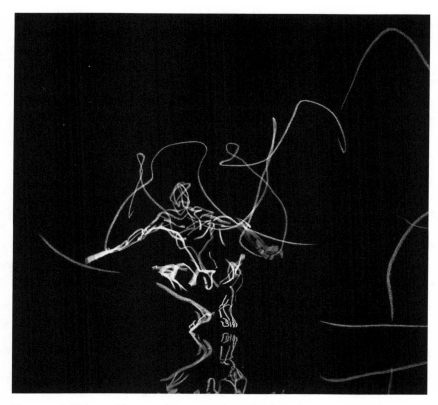

Figure 5. Still from *Ghostcatching*, 1999, by Bill T. Jones, Paul Kaiser, and Shelley Eshkar. Image courtesy of Kaiser/Eshkar.

At one point, Jones hums a child's song that he sang earlier in the show: "Go Tell Aunt Rhody. Go Tell Aunt Rhody. Go Tell Aunt Rhody—the old grey goose is dead." Later, Jones sings an even more sinister and otherworldly song: "I'd fly away to the one I love." Figures appear and get caught, but traces remain. All the while we hear Jones's voice, deep, low, and strange.

As the piece ends, seven sticklike figures emerge, resembling the original caged image. They move as though bound within a blue web, roped with blue wire. They lunge out with weighted force but are caught, resembling a group of people moving in a chain gang. Bound, they cannot get very far. At the end, confined, they remain blue and lurching.

In *The Breathing Show,* the juxtaposition of live and digital bodies is immediately compelling. How do *Ghostcatching*'s blue figures relate to the real-life Jones, who has a casual relationship with the audience, taking time after his vigorously danced solos to wipe his brow with a towel, drink some water, and chat with the audience with all the confidence and style expected from him? Jones quite consciously inserted these improvised transitions into the evening's events. By contrasting the mediated figure in *Ghostcatching* and the live, improvising Jones, I do not mean to ignore the many ways that the live and the mediated imbricate each other. Nor do I mean to embrace the modernist trap of suggesting that the sweating, chatting Jones is simplistically more "real" or "authentic" than the digital body. To be sure, even Jones's casual persona is a performed character, sometimes enacted quite (self-)consciously. When discussing his early years dancing with Zane in Binghamton, Jones illustrates this type of performance by stating, "We had public personas like suits of clothes that we put on, or were somehow put on for us."[39] As much as any dancer in history, people expect things of Jones: dynamism, outspokenness, and politicization. Either in keeping with or against these expectations, he performs.

Granting the shifting and performative nature of the self that Jones presents on stage, important distinctions nevertheless exist between his live and mediated forms as presented in *The Breathing Show.* Particularly interesting, and politically important, is the virtual figure's inability to sweat or lose its breath like the live and fleshy Jones. This juxtaposition exists at the very foundation of the *Ghostcatching* collaboration. When Jones joined Kaiser and Eshkar in the motion-capture studio, he had twenty-four markers affixed to his body as he danced in a studio full of lights, cameras, and screens. Doubtful whether the new technology could actually capture the subtle nuances of his quivers and undulations, Jones nevertheless began improvising. According to Paul Kaiser, "Six times he ran through the series, each improvisation freer and more fluid than the last. As his exuberance took over, the sweat poured out of him and some of the markers popped off of him."[40] Discussing the early limitations and frustrations in the motion-capture studio, Jones describes the space as being cold with a hard floor, less than ideal conditions for a dancer's body. More important, he echoes Kaiser in stating, "They hadn't really thought out the limitations of the sensors on my body. . . . Sure enough, once I began to sweat [the sensors] would pop off and then everything would stop. . . . And I said, 'I don't think your technology can actually capture what I do.' "[41] This is a profound claim, suggesting a moment from *The History of Sexuality, Volume 2,* where Foucault announces, "It is not that life has been totally integrated into techniques that govern and administer it; it constantly escapes them."[42] Sweat and the new technology repelled each other from the beginning of the *Ghostcatching* project. The material outpouring of Jones's work actually stopped the motion of production.

Jones was eventually impressed by the truth of the "dots swirling around on the computer screen," mesmerized by the fact that they presented his movement on a screen despite the absence of his "body." Nevertheless, there is very little trace, if any, of his labor, his improvisational exhaustion, once *Ghostcatching* becomes fully realized as a public work. Unlike the virtual image, unable to fatigue, the sweat of Jones's live dancing body creates exuberance, providing material evidence of his recent labor and physical exertion. While admittedly not all labor is sweated and not all sweat is labor, an undeniable gap emerges between the two figures, one digital and the other live. Making this gap visible has racialized, political ramifications of interest to Jones. Rather than bow graciously and then disappear behind the curtain, Jones talks with the audience, making audible his body's rapid pulse and need for breath.

In *No Respect: Intellectuals and Popular Culture,* Andrew Ross discusses various images of work on stage. In reference to jazz musicians, he argues that the "spectacle of work," visibly signified by sweat on the brow, contains multiple meanings that interrupt romantic images of the spontaneous, virtuoso master of leisure on stage: "It is the sweat of the vestigial minstrel clown, but is also the reminder of the sweat of slave labor . . . a comforting reminder to a white audience that labor exists, and is elsewhere, in a black body. But it is also a militant negation of the racist stereotype of the 'lazy' i.e. underemployed black male."[43] By contrast, Ross states that "in the 'cool' world of modern jazz ushered in by bebop, evidence of strenuous activity is supposed to be interpreted as a sign of mental and not physical labor."[44] And, of course, this shunning of the physical has its own racial history.

But Jones is a black male dancer, master of an art where beauty and virtuosity are tied inseparably to the physical. What now does one make of the unabashedly sweating Bill T. Jones, an iconic figure in the dance world known for his identity-centered work, placed up against his motion-captured image, dancing without sweat and skin? While the virtual motion-captured figure itself has no sweat or racial markings, its juxtaposition with the live

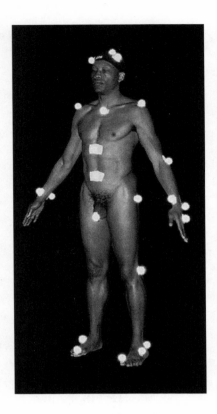

Figure 6. Bill T. Jones wearing motion-
capture markers. Image courtesy of
Kaiser/Eshkar.

improvising Jones invigorates their absence in a way that challenges any simple celebration or comfort that the audience might take in the slick, blue images. Not only does one remember Jones when one sees the virtual movement, but one hears his voice at various points, making it impossible to shut
out remembrances of the fleshy body, black and working.

Automatons, Labor, and the Racialized Other

The absence of sweat in a virtual image of a black dancing body recalls a long
history of relationships between imaging technologies and the working body.
Francis Barker, a professor of literature at the University of Essex, has a dark
view of man's fascination with automatons, claiming that notions of artificial
man have haunted the individual throughout modernity: "It [the automaton]

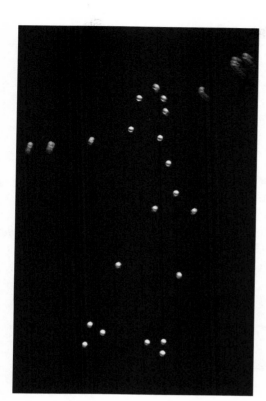

Fig. 7. Step 3: Markers
optically recorded and
converted to digital 3D files.
Image courtesy of
Kaiser/Eshkar.

appears in our peripheral vision; in our dreams and nightmares; our psyches,
in our films, and in our philosophy, and so on. And it appears not as the romantic 'other' of our normality, but as the question of the normative itself."[45]
He argues that, historically, automatons have fundamentally challenged
closely guarded notions of human authenticity. Considering *Ghostcatching*,
dance scholar Kent DeSpain voices similar anxiety by asking: "How will we
define what is human and what is not in an era of increasingly extensive and
invasive biotechnology? Will what is imaginable on a computer become what
is demanded on a stage, and will the dancers who try to fulfill that vision be
forced to resort to more and more medical assistance to improve or repair
their overtaxed bodies?"[46] DeSpain echoes Barker's claims regarding the anxiety brought on by automatons throughout modernity: how do we maintain
our sense of the human in the face of increasingly sophisticated technological

mappings of and abstractions from the body? In addition, De Spain expresses the fear of failing, exhausted, "overtaxed" bodies, a condition common in both factory workers and dancers, albeit in different ways.

In discussing the history of automatons, scholars frequently note the famous creations of the sixteenth to eighteenth centuries: Jacques de Vaucanson's gilt-brass duck that not only quacked and waddled like a real duck but above all made its internal digestive processes visible; or *The Musician*, by Pierre Jaquet-Droz, which amazed audiences in 1773 with its mechanical woman who played a miniature clavichord by pressing her fingers upon the keys. Allen Feldman has recently added to this rich scholarship on reproductions of everyday life by conducting an insightful archaeology linking automatons, labor, and the senses. In his essay "The Human Touch: Towards a Historical Anthropology and Dream Analysis of Self-Acting Instruments," dance and labor bear a relationship from the very first sentence, which describes Father Athanasius Kircher's seventeenth-century diagram of an automated water organ. On the right side of the organ, automatons made to look like blacksmiths are hard at work with their hands; on the left side, grotesque figures dance a dance of death.[47]

While figures resembling humans initially thrilled people, mechanized figures performing human tasks fascinated them even more. A model that could play the piano realistically, or a miniature piano that could play a real piece of music without any figure whatsoever, pleased and intrigued people, with a twinge of the anxiety noted by Barker. By the eighteenth century, which Feldman takes to be the classical age for automaton design, mechanized figures became increasingly miniaturized, so that by the nineteenth century they made their way from the courts and exhibit halls of Europe to the domestic space of the bourgeois parlor. They became decorous, household curios. Given the remarkable shifts that came with the age of mechanical reproduction, these "curios" also created metaphors for real workers in the factory, thus collapsing factory, worker, and product into one. In short, automatons provided the spectacle of mechanical labor, complete except for the individual. Feldman suggests that by teaching its audience how to play with machines, the automaton relieved the pressure or burden of labor, making it an aesthetic product of consumption.

During the nineteenth century, anxiety about fatigue and economic production arose. Of course, Karl Marx is the most famous chronicler and theorist of these nineteenth-century changes. In volume 1 of *Das Kapital,* first published in 1867, Marx discusses the many changes in labor brought about by the machine. He explains the ironic fact that "the most powerful instrument for reducing labor-time suffers a dialectical inversion and becomes the most unfailing means of turning the whole lifetime of the worker and his family into labor-time at capital's disposal for its own valorization."[48] Machines had the capacity to increase a worker's productivity while also eliminating the backbreaking nature of manual labor. Marx cites the cotton gin (1793), which enabled a worker to go from separating and cleaning one pound of cotton per day to one hundred pounds, presumably without the same strain. But, Marx argues, instead of relieving workers, these machines made it possible for anyone and everyone, including women and children, to join the workforce and enabled the workday to be stretched beyond natural limits. This, he notes, is the gruesome paradox of capitalism in the age of machines: "It creates, on the one hand, new conditions which permit capital to give free rein to this tendency, and on the other hand, new incentives which whet its insatiable appetite for the labor of others."[49] And since the machine does not fatigue, it could seemingly go on producing forever were it not for the limits of its human operators, which become pushed to extremes.

Still trying to figure out why people in this age of industrial production derided by Marx were so fascinated by indefatigable mechanical automatons, Feldman notes that the utopian image of automatons appeared mainly in the privacy and security of the middle class, far from the concrete class tensions and the physical stress of the factory floor.[50] According to Anson Rabinach, "The production ideologies of the nineteenth century understood the physical limits of the laboring body, particularly the body under the stress and strain of industrial mass production, as a moral horizon that set the practical limits of civilizational progress."[51] If capital was the way to progress, fatigue provided an obstacle. This is precisely the problem noted by Marx. In addition, Feldman argues that fatigue and exhaustion in the factory were linked not only to broad social breakdown but also to "the uncontrollable and involuntary release of irrational behavior and sexual drives that were antithetical to the public morality of the work ethic and the private morality of bourgeois decorum."[52] The bourgeoisie feared the activities that the working class engaged in to let off steam, activities like sex and alcohol consumption that supposedly represented a fall into the realm of mere instinct. According to Feldman, the automatons offered a perfect view of labor that had no need for these "uncontrollable" behaviors. Feldman also proposes that automa-

tons in some instances appeared to the working class as images of moral uplift: figures that work unceasingly, without the need to rest or recuperate.[53]
The fact that automatons were immune to the usual fatigues of labor implied
that the mere humans who were not were somehow guilty of moral faltering.

Furthermore, the technology of eighteenth- and nineteenth-century automatons was often aestheticized precisely by images of the colonial subject.
According to Feldman:

> There were the Swiss automata that depicted anthropomorphic, ape-like,
> Negroid fiddlers, or the automated, moving, and musical elephant
> mounted by a brown skinned Hindu mahout. There was a whole series of
> Orientalist automata: soothsayers magicians, and conjurers such as the
> Chinese magician sitting in a temple or a music box showing a magician
> in Persian dress flanked by two monkey musicians in Asiatic costume
> playing cellos and violin. There were the Arab tightrope dancer with
> black musicians playing drums; the Indian snake charmer who played
> clockwork music through a flute; the Negro dressed in slave garb; another
> Negroid narghile smoker, dressed in Egyptian costume, with exaggerated
> lips drinking a cup of coffee; an automaton of a westernized Negro being
> shaved; and that of a black crossbowman wearing nothing but a loin
> cloth made of palm leaves.[54]

Interestingly, the Industrial Revolution did not end man's fascination
with automata. Instead, graphic images and photographic recordings
emerged to map the body in detail, with labor figuring into the equation ever
more explicitly. During the 1860s, Étienne-Jules Marey, professor of the "natural history of organized bodies" at the Collège de France, began investigat-
ing the movement of bodies. "'From the invisible atom to the celestial body
lost in space,' he wrote, 'everything is subject to motion.'"[55] Initially, he used
a graphing device with one end attached to a moving object and the other attached to a stylus that inscribed the moving object's fluctuations onto strips
of paper covered with soot. Since the object needed to be attached to the
graphing tool, these graphing devices were limited in what they could
record.[56]

Later, having seen Eadward Muybridge's photographs of galloping horses
in an 1878 issue of the journal *La Nature,* Marey began corresponding with
Muybridge and embarked on his own photographic studies.[57] Marey sought
new photographic methods to capture the principles underlying movement, as
opposed to merely representing it. With these experiments in mind, people of-

ten cite Marey as the earliest and most direct precursor to the motion-capture technology used by Paul Kaiser and Shelley Eshkar in their collaboration with Bill T. Jones. While the recent digital work done in 1999 is clearly much more sophisticated than Marey's work, the two started from similar places, and the visual images from both processes are strikingly similar.

Although Marey developed a wide range of techniques in seeking movement's underlying principles, the one most related to the recent work with motion capture was called chronophotography. Here, Marey clothed his subject entirely in black with the exception of thin white bands or bright metal buttons strategically attached to the body.[58] Marey would then photograph the moving figure against a black interior, thereby capturing only the movements of the strips, making visible what he considered the essential components of movement. Marey went on to replace the strips and buttons with tiny lights to create photographic images with greater precision. Used to study the movements of soldiers and patients in Parisian hospitals, Marey's techniques captured movement without the distractions caused by the exterior of a subject's body. Marey aimed to reveal the invisible movement behind or beyond the visible moving body, a desire that we hear echoed and complicated in Jones's recent return to form.

The visual similarities between Marey's motion-capture experiments and those of Kaiser/Eshkar with Jones are striking. And although a century stands between early experiments with chronophotography and recent work with motion capture, Paul Kaiser's aims resemble Marey's attempt to capture movement without the "distractions" of the subject's fleshy, or visible, body. When asked by Kent De Spain whether we were moving into an era of posthuman dance, Kaiser responded by distancing his motion-capture works from dance. He claimed that these works were more about drawing, unable to replace the "ecstasy and the immediacy of live dancers."[59] Kaiser went on to say that with motion capture's ability to abstract dance from its physical basis, "it's moving away [from the physical basis of the performer] . . . and I think that might clean out our eyes in many ways. I think that in looking at performers on the stage we are seduced by the charisma of the body rather than by the beauty of the movement."[60]

The beauty of human movement fascinated Marey, Kaiser, and Eshkar, especially when abstracted from bodily "distractions." It is problematic, however, that Kaiser so easily links bodily distractions with "charisma." As I have already stated, Jones's labor as well as his skin have been "ghosted,"

Fig. 8. Georges Demeny dressed in black in preparation for geometric chronophotography, 1884. Image courtesy of Marta Braun.

Fig 9. Exposure showing Marey's motion-capture suit markers.

two things clearly bound together but also bound with Jones's so-called charisma. As part of Arlene Croce's ongoing feud with Jones, Croce accused him in 1995 of having let his "charisma" get the better of him, blinding him to the pitfalls of identity-centered work. Regarding what she calls the "permissiveness" of art in the 1960s and the "invidious logic at work in the campaigns of the multiculturalists, the moral guardians, and the minority groups," Croce remarks, "Jones, caught up in his own charisma, didn't seem to hear the trap being sprung."[61] According to Marey, and Kaiser one hundred years later, race and labor had to be removed in order to "clean our eyes out" and get at the "beauty of pure movement."

Tight Places and Images of Confinement

Of course, Jones didn't want to be a "a disembodied, denatured, de-gendered series of lines moving in a void."[62] He wanted to challenge the so-called freedom of abstracted movement, the imagined pure neutrality of form. By strategically revealing his sweat and skin throughout *The Breathing Show,* he uniquely challenges previous mechanized commodifications of the body. In addition, his pointed banter with the audience forces so-called abstraction into a consideration of race and politics. Early in *The Breathing Show*, having danced for several minutes to music by Franz Schubert, Jones exclaims, "Anyway, this is where I'm supposed to swing into this thing about why I'm dancing to this dead European man's music."[63] There's laughter, and Jones, promising that it won't be "one of those evenings," discusses a painter friend who introduced Jones to Schubert's music. Having engaged with the music deeply for a choreographic project not long afterward, Jones claims, "I realized that I was a romantic—that was my problem." Laughter emerges from the audience. "When Arnie and I came to the scene in the late seventies, it was certainly not a romantic scene and I didn't know what to do. . . . But now I have come out as a Romantic." Applause and laughter erupt, given the loaded phrase "come out" used triumphantly and with a twist. But really, this discussion is all about Jones's supposed controversial turn to form. Jones then wonders aloud about the place of black Americans during Schubert's time: "Just to play with myself, I started to think: What would I have been like in 1830? What would I have been dancing like? I certainly wouldn't be here. . . . What would it have sounded like?"

And with that, instead of the Schubert recordings blasting through the speakers, Jones sings "Go Tell Aunt Rhody," the children's song he later sings in *Ghostcatching*—a sonic reference to racism and slavery in America, linking the live Jones with his virtual image. Jones punctuates the verses with stomping, undulating, quite musical phrases of movement. Some of his steps are narrative, seeming to illustrate or interpret the lyrics. In other cases, they insert music into the breaks, referencing vernacular styles. Meanwhile, the dancing affects the sound of the voice as we hear Jones's need for breath and as we hear the stomps and leaps manifest in the juttings of his voice. He finishes the song not vocally, but with arms outstretched, head back, and mouth open. The final Schubert dance then begins, having been punctuated by a different sound, a live sound from the dancing Jones, danced and sung in resonance with a black radical tradition emerging out of slavery.

Following *The Breathing Show*'s 1999 premiere in Iowa City, Jones toured the piece through Europe. At that time, he was worried about the show's quality and continued to rework its contents for the looming New York showing. In his journal entries from that time, Jones writes: "I use improvisation because it catches me at my most animal, most un-self-conscious and most bold. . . . Here is my truest contribution to contemporary dance."[64]

In keeping with this realization, Jones discovered that improvised breaks, when he could sing and chat and reveal his personality, were essential to the piece. Only with these improvised moments did the piece begin to "come alive." On tour, Jones inserted *Floating the Tongue* into the program, suggesting that his improvised journey of 1978—intensely personal and political—still plays a vital part in his dance investigations. With *Floating the Tongue* appearing on the heels of *Ghostcatching,* the result was a challenging juxtaposition, vitally questioning the freedom of digital abstraction from the body.

Equally important are *Ghostcatching*'s images of confinement, indexing the historical criminalization of black mobility. In an interview with Kent De-Spain, Paul Kaiser refers to the figures that emerge as "spawns," a term also used by Jones. These spawns break free only to get reabsorbed by the initial figure. According to Kaiser, "It's all about the notion of breaking free from your own representation, and being caught up in it again."[65] The piece suggests the impossibility of breaking free—from one's own representation but also from real confining spaces. The fact that the figure always gets "caught up in it again" troubles any simple celebration of freedom and mobility. As the piece progresses, the spawns that move with any sense of space and freedom end up frozen amid their blue traces.

Perhaps the blue traces and boundaries surrounding Bill T. Jones and his virtual spawns can be better explained through the idea of "tight spaces," which Houston Baker developed in *Turning South Again.* As I explained in my introduction, Baker uses the phrase to raise the questions "Who moves? Who doesn't?" Historically, the black man hasn't been able to move (to say nothing of the black woman). Mobility for African American men has been criminalized, most viciously under the Southern slave system but in a host of other situations as well. Describing black slaves' legal status in the American South, Baker references the legal scholar and jurist Leon Higginbotham, who explains that blacks were forbidden from leaving their owners' plantations without certification, thereby destroying their freedom of mobility. Beyond that, their ability to resist was seriously diminished by the fact that they were liable to be severely punished (if not killed outright) for challenging a Christian in any way and were also of course prohibited from carrying arms.[66] Baker argues that while modernism was exemplified by Walter Benjamin's publicly mobile flâneur, a "mobile, observant, multiply personalitied city wanderer," this modernity was denied to the black masses. Baker goes on to argue, "The identity dilemma for the black majority is not captured by the declarative 'one ever feels his two-ness,' but rather by the interrogative 'how do I break these all-too-real chains binding me?' "[67]

In *Last Night on Earth*, Jones laments: "I think that even those of us who have no notion of what the auction block was can still feel it, as if the memory of it is handed down to us through our mother's milk. . . . It is there with me when I dance before you on a stage."[68] When seen in the context of this history, *Ghostcatching*'s blue images of confinement ring all the more forcefully. As for the absence of skin, in discussing the prohibition of mobility under slavery, Baker notes: "The body's natural 'color' was converted into a legalized marker of oppression. There was, in the total institution called slavery, an *epidermalization* of oppression. Skin color—in combination with facial features and hair texture—became southern grounds for maintenance of the ideological and economic project of White Supremacy."[69] While one's various identity claims—racial, ethnic, class, religious, gender, sexuality, place, generation—by no means fit tidily along clear color lines, *racism* is nevertheless largely a visual pathology.

Unlike Jones, Paul Gilroy likely would embrace *Ghostcatching* as further evidence that we have already moved to a point where vision-based race thinking is out of date. His controversial book *Against Race*, published in 2000, has infuriated many scholars with its call to eliminate liberal race-based thinking in the hopes of a humanism that would manage to move beyond the color line. Most relevant to *Ghostcatching* is Gilroy's claim that new technologies, particularly in the medical field, have begun to transform what he calls "the old, modern representational economies that reproduced 'race' subdermally and epidermally."[70] He argues that advancements in molecular biology, which show that race is genetically virtually insignificant, as well as the development of imaging technologies such as ultrasound and electromagnetic radiation, have enabled new forms of scrutiny regarding the human body. Gilroy asks: "Have you, has your body, your child's body, ever been scanned? Do you recognize its changing optic density? If so, perhaps you could consider that development another compelling sign that we have begun to let the old visual signatures of 'race' go."[71]

A few pages later, engaging head-on with what Baker describes as the historical epidermalization of oppression whereby skin color became the grounds for white supremacy, Gilroy claims: "Today skin is no longer privileged as the threshold of either identity or particularity. There are good reasons to suppose that the line between inside and out now falls elsewhere. The boundaries of 'race' have moved across the threshold of the skin. They are cellular and molecular, not dermal. If 'race' is to endure, it will be in a new form, estranged from the scales respectively associated with political anatomy and epidermalization."[72]

While motion capture is undoubtedly part of a range of new technologies that enable new mappings and forms of scrutiny regarding the body, these advancements in technology have done little if anything to alter the general public's conception of the human body. We are a long way from realizing a utopian humanism in these increasingly fluid borders. It is in this context that Bill T. Jones stood in front of students at NYU, asking, "Are we past a point of racial looking? Why can't *I* be free?"[73] At the same talk, Jones told the students that the first thing he did upon entering the packed auditorium, without even thinking, was to look around to count the number of black faces in the audience. One could say that Jones was speaking from a tight place, especially regarding his supposed turn to form. He wants to foreground the how of dance, and yet he constantly reminds us of the stakes involved. He seems frustrated with the onus of always foregrounding the political, and yet he is a black man dancing. At one moment, he professes an interest in turns and pointed feet, while a moment later he sings "We Shall Overcome." It is from this tight place that Jones calls for his doubling: "Can you see with two sets of eyes?" It is also from this tight place that Jones, together with Kaiser and Eshkar, created *Ghostcatching,* which, especially when shown as part of *The Breathing Show*, challenges the "freedom" and beauty of motion abstracted from bodily "distractions."

Ghostcatching within *The Breathing Show* ushers both a warning and a call to dance audiences, especially important as motion capture and other digital abstractions from the body become more prevalent. It would be a great loss to reduce Bill T. Jones to a black choreographer, a gay choreographer, or whatever mark of difference one chooses. André Lepecki refers to such reduction as a prison, built out of guilt and a lack of imagination.[74] With movement that comes from many places—from laborers, Trisha, Arnie, his mother—Jones moves between constructions of difference, neither stable nor essential.

That being said, Jones makes clear the fact that we are not in a world beyond difference, outside of history. Back at the beginning of his career, he broke from the utopian claims of contact improvisation and other postmod-

ern experiments invested in the notion of "pure" movement. He forced audiences to realize the limits and blind spots of claims that movement could
ever be mere exercises with nothing at stake. Similarly today, even as he becomes increasingly interested in the how of dance, Jones points to the limits
of motion-capture technology and asks us not to embrace its liberatory potential too quickly. To Bill T. Jones, form is never neutral and removed from
politics. He urges audiences to view dance doubly. And finally, however
beautiful the resulting movement may be, Jones suggests that the act of
"cleaning out one's eyes" by wiping away markers of difference could easily
become a brutal hygiene.

Conclusion: Exquisite Dancing—Altering the Terrain of Tight Places

In each of this book's four chapters, I have highlighted many of the social, historical, and formal constraints that affect how people move, paying particular attention to the tight places that celebrations of improvised dance frequently fail to notice. Although I believe that this is necessary work, I also want to make sure not to obscure the many ways in which the actual dancing is amazing—even though it is hard for words to illuminate or adequately pay tribute to the moments of eloquence, ferocity, speed, and lines of flight that inspired and continue to animate this study. Early in this project, as one way to limit the book's case studies, I decided to write only about improvised dancing that I wanted to spend time watching. Now, having spent many attentive hours with videos, photographs, sound recordings, and live performances, I have been moved far more, and far differently, than I ever anticipated. And I want to sit the reader down and say: *Watch* this. *Listen* to this. Does it make you feel like *dancing*?

In this respect, I feel a certain kinship with the dance writer Julie Taylor. In the course of writing *Paper Tangos,* her book about studying tango in Buenos Aires amid the terror of military dictatorships, Taylor grappled with how to convey tango's rich knowledge on the written page. How can one possibly translate the subtleties of dance, a moving bodily art, into words? In the book's first chapter, entitled "Choreographing a Paper Tango," Taylor explains the challenge of giving dance adequate presence in the text. Wanting to give the reader a sense of the dancing she had come to love, Taylor notes numerous moments of dancing and highlights fleeting observations such as "the eloquence of the woman's legs, rising and falling like breathing."[1] In the end, Taylor selected small still images from the film *Tango: The Exile of Gardel,* by Fernando Solanas, to include on the bottom right edge of each page. Flipping through the book, one sees these images dance. A man and a woman, locked in a noble embrace, circle around each other as one turns the book's first twenty pages. Later, loose papers flutter down the center of a circular staircase—appropriate for Taylor's "paper tangos" but also corresponding to the memories and associations that gathered around her experience as a dancer in Buenos Aires. The book's final pages reveal yet another couple, this time in an atmosphere both dusky and austere. The background is dark, and the dance floor has the warm glow of wood captured on black and white film. As one turns the pages, the dancers' legs intertwine and release in intricate designs, and the partners alternate in taking swift jumps, lilting upon eloquent pockets of air.

With the exception of a few significant photographs, this book lacks such concrete visual imagery. Still, I empathize with Taylor's desire to convey and honor the moments of dancing she came to love. If this book contained a flipbook, it undoubtedly would include certain moments from *The Palladium: Where Mambo Was King*. In one sequence of startling eloquence, Millie Donay, a regular at the Palladium, wears a white mermaid-style dress, slim through the bodice and hips, accentuating her curves and subtle swings, with fabric unfurling just below her thighs. With a clear sense of *clave*, Donay swivels her hips in smooth counterpoint to the direction of her knees, with one arm gracefully arriving atop her head. Then, circling around her partner, she catches air and lands in her improbably high shoes, as if on a floor made of felt. Her gorgeous, yet understated, hopping appears to take place in slow motion, revealing elegance and eloquence in equal amplitude. And of course, one cannot ignore her partner, "Cuban Pete," and the clarity and speed with which he extends one of his famously long legs in front of his body, with a moment of accented stillness, before slowly pulling it back.

The flipbook would also include moments from Dianne McIntyre's improvised solo, *Etude in Free,* created two years after her performance with Max Roach and Abbey Lincoln and clearly an extension of that work. The video recording of *Etude in Free* highlights McIntyre's female form, clearly aged since her early improvisations and wearing iconic accoutrements that signify gender. Whereas most documentation of McIntyre's work exists in black and white footage, here she dances in full color, in a shiny pink leotard and pink stirrup tights. She wears her hair down, adorned with a pink ribbon. The camera swirls around her, frequently cutting her off, at times so close that it obscures her movement. But the camera's closeness reveals McIn-

tyre sweating through her pink makeup. She wears hoop earrings and a dis-
concerting pink ribbon around her throat, disturbing in its simultaneous
daintiness and collarlike constraint. Her throat pushes against the ribbon
every time she arches backward. And here the limits of the flipbook emerge,
for the exquisite nature of McIntyre's improvised work demands a sound
score as well. This book's critical work depends upon the improvised sounds
of Bill Dixon's horn and the devastating music of Abbey Lincoln's screams.

In addition, there are the clunky moments in *Fall after Newton,* where
dancers hurl themselves at one another, only to find a missed connection, and
the angular, unplanned but compelling, fall onto the floor. There are the stunning moments where Nancy Stark Smith's long braided hair swings through
the air as she spins behind Curt Siddall's neck, moving horizontally from
shoulder to shoulder. She's a thinking dancer, who wants to say no more often, who recognizes the value and occasional need to use one's body as an obstruction. There is Steve Paxton's elegant walk, and dancers engaged in "The
Stand"—taking time for a physical practice that might look like nothing but
in fact involves the expansion of choices and physical possibility. And here
another soundtrack emerges: "I Want to Be Ready," from Ailey's *Revelations,* which underscores all of these improvised falls.

And of course there is Bill T. Jones: the point in *The Breathing Show*
where he stretches his arms outward to form a T that seems to extend from
his chest to the farthest reaches of the stage. There's the deep resonant sound
of his voice singing "Go Tell Aunt Rhody," interrupted by stomps and the
most elegant undulations. There's the moment in his improvised banter with
the audience when, in the midst of applause, he closes his eyes, raises his left
arm, and stomps three times, spontaneously reaffirming the celebration.
There's the quiver, both slight and brave, as Jones rises to relevé in *Floating
the Tongue,* releasing a series of spoken associations both personal and political: "What does it mean to be an adult? To own property? . . . Open me
up, oh lord, open my heart . . . I'm sweating."[2]

While long, this list of extraordinary moments is by no means exhaustive.
Moreover, while I include these descriptions out of love, and a desire to pay
tribute to the dancers' skill, it is important to point out that these exquisite
moments are not reducible to some imagined apolitical realm of aesthetics.
They are exquisite in that they reveal bravery, and choice, and surprise, and
trust, and often a keen aesthetic sense of form, all of which are particularly
poignant when understood as erupting out of, and in relation to, a variety of

tight places. I have tried to suggest throughout the book that the *practice* of improvisation—the training that truly skillful improvisation requires—is a rigorous mode of making oneself ready for a range of potential situations. It is an incessant preparation, grounded in the present while open to the next moment's possible actions and constraints. According to this logic, even when there is no "exquisite" moment, no clear arrival or climax, the practice of improvisation is politically powerful as a mode of making oneself ready. This is the way in which improvisation pushes against static reifications of freedom.

Still, the wondrous quality of the moments described here cannot be ignored. They suggest that improvised dance offers more than a method of coping with the world's tight places, a mere survival strategy in which one is always on the run. Undeniably, improvisation and survival are often vitally linked, which constitutes an important part of improvisation's necessity and political power. Figuring out how to move (or not) in a moment of violent confrontation (as in the Freedom Rides), or in an unfamiliar situation of physical duress (as in the case of an unexpected fall), or as a person of color in a newly integrated dance hall, or as the only black woman in a university program in modern dance, are not things to be taken lightly. There are many tight places where a failure to figure out how to move has damaging, if not dire, consequences. Unfortunately, there are times when no degree of improvisational skill is sufficient to extract oneself from a situation of duress. But, as I've said before, if this were always the case, one could easily see the exhausting "burden of improvisation." The exquisite moments described earlier suggest that there is more to the story. They attest to a political potential beyond survival. To riff on Ralph Ellison's words, improvised dance is often about finding a way to "move without moving."[3] But beyond that, it is about doing so *creatively*, without surrendering one's agency. It is about moving where movement might not have seemed possible or in a way that, for whatever reason, no one could have imagined prior to its realization.

Bill Dixon describes the importance of improvisational creativity like this: "There is an ambience; either man-made that might consist of those things heard (and out there) whether one wanted their presence or not, or the other ambience that one made oneself, that had more to do with what one wanted to have oneself surrounded by. And that's what made the idea and reality of improvisation so important."[4] Dixon recognizes that the world-making potential of improvisation involves the ability to make new spaces, to create and form one's surroundings continually, as one would wish them to be. Rather than merely accept the world as it is given, musicians such as Dixon strove to create through improvisation a more desirable setting in which to live. Even when the result appears playful, this world-making improvisation differs from mere fantasy or escape. As Dixon said, this is what made the "idea *and the reality* of improvisation so important."[5]

Although Michel Foucault never writes about dance explicitly, his late interviews help to explain the political power of improvised dance—illuminating how improvisation, a practice intimately concerned with constraint, still relates to freedom. For readers primarily familiar with Foucault's early work, this would seem an unlikely claim. Early on, he analyzed and tried to disarm the objective status of human sciences such as biology, economics, linguistics, and psychiatry. He revealed how domination and subjugation course through society's apparently rational disciplines and institutions. Then, he began to analyze not only the human sciences but also the disciplinary practices of the nineteenth century and the ways in which modern power operates. His work directly challenged the apparent benevolence of humanism, exposing the insidious ways in which power both controls and creates the modern subject. Power seemed to be everywhere, difficult to wield and even more difficult to resist. Foucault described a social and political landscape much akin to a world of tight spaces, rife with shifting constraints. Readers, particularly in the United States, read this work as deeply pessimistic, for there seemed to be no room for escape.

Foucault's stance, however, was not so simple. As Alexander Nehamas notes in *The Art of Living: Socratic Reflections from Plato to Foucault,* "As early as 1961 Michel Serres had noticed something very important in *Folie et déraison,* which, according to Serres, was not simply a scientific treatise on madness but 'also a cry.'"[6] Foucault was deeply attuned to and affected by suffering in the world. According to Serres and Nehamas, although Foucault offered no solutions to the plight he described, a deep love nevertheless circulated in his early work.[7] Then, in the early 1970s, Foucault began to work on *The History of Sexuality.* Between the introductory volume and the next two, his entire approach seemed to shift. Still interested in the wide range of power relations present in human relationships, ranging from politics to family life to romantic affairs to pedagogical situations, Foucault argued that power relations are "mobile, reversible, and unstable."[8]

This glimpse of mobility is where Foucault's thinking applies to improvised dance and the tight places discussed in the previous chapters. Although perhaps Mario Bauzá initially was intimidated by the Palladium's management (one can't know for sure), one can imagine a shifting power dynamic once the Blen Blen Club brought in tons of money. Or, a complacent viewer, at ease in watching Dianne McIntyre dance, might shift significantly upon hearing Abbey Lincoln scream. Or, although the Judson Dance Theater seemed democratic to some people in Greenwich Village, their performances likely would have played differently uptown. According to Foucault's late work, the challenge is to determine where resistance will develop and the form it will take. He argues that each instance of domination has distinct contours and requires a specific response.

Of course, Foucault admits that there are certain states of domination where, through economic, political, or military means, "an individual or social group succeeds in blocking a field of power relations, immobilizing them and preventing any reversibility of movement."[9] In these cases, there is very little space or room for freedom. In the very tightest situations of domination, where movement is almost entirely blocked, some form of liberation is necessary. Still, as I mentioned in the introduction, Foucault argues that one must be careful when speaking of "liberation." He explains that often when people advocate liberation, they mistakenly assume that all will be well if they can break very specific sets of chains; they assume that with liberation, man will resume a positive relationship with himself and return to his natural free state. For Foucault, while liberation is often urgent and necessary, it is never sufficient for creating a full form of existence. He therefore emphasizes the need for "practices of freedom."

In the years leading up to his death in 1984, Foucault became increasingly interested in how these practices could operate within a world that in so many ways seems to be the opposite of "free." In the process, he became inspired by an imperative found in ancient ethical philosophy: care for yourself. Amazingly, the ancient understanding of "care" had everything to do with both a mental and a physical kind of preparation. Foucault explains in "Technologies of the Self": "[The principal features of this care] include exercises [both mental and physical] in which the subject puts himself in a situation in which he can verify whether he can confront events and use the discourses with which he is armed. It is a question of testing the preparation."[10] Foucault talks about both meditations, where one imagines possible responses to various events, and ambulatory exercises (gymnasia), where one literally goes for a walk in order to test one's reactions. Foucault refers to both of these ancient preparatory exercises as improvisations, meaningful in themselves.[11]

Although Foucault by no means idealizes antiquity, he maintains that care for self is necessary for practices of freedom, which involve an ongoing stylization of the self where one both respects the constraints of reality and tries to violate them. Here, Foucault began to think of technologies of the self as an art of living: "What strikes me is the fact that, in our society, art has become something that is related only to objects and not to individuals or to life. That art is something which is specialized or done by experts who are artists. But couldn't everyone's life become a work of art? Why should the lamp or the house be an art object, but not our life?"[12] Nehamas notes that art, with the flimsy notions of unlimited freedom and absolute spontaneity that surround it, would seem an unlikely model for Foucauldian ethics, especially for those familiar with Foucault's early work. However, Nehamas suggests: "In the end there is no contradiction. For creativity, too, is always historically situated. Not everything is possible at every time. Like everyone else, artists have to work within the limitations of their traditions. . . . Lives, seen aesthetically, are no different."[13]

In a description of practices of freedom that very much resembles improvised dance, Foucault explains:

> [If] we are not to settle for the affirmation or the empty dream of freedom, it seems to me that this historico-critical attitude must also be an experimental one. I mean that this work done at the limits of ourselves must, on the one hand, open up a realm of historical inquiry, and, on the other, put itself to a test of reality, of contemporary reality, both to grasp the points where change is possible and desirable, and to determine the precise form this change should take.[14]

Although the work involved in practices of freedom could (and should) take a variety of forms, it entails precisely the same work as improvised dance. As I have argued throughout the book, skilled improvisers become intimately acquainted with constraint, figuring out in the moment what is desirable and what is possible to change. Perhaps most important for studies of improvised dance, Foucault argues that practices of freedom and care for self ought not be reduced to self-indulgence, entertainment, or mere leisure activity. It would be a mistake to reduce improvised dance to the realm of "entertainment" or a separate sphere of "art." In *Discipline and Punish,* Foucault discusses the need to write a history of punishment against the background of a history of bodies, because "it is always the body that is at issue." He continues, "The body is . . . directly involved in a political field; power relations have an immediate hold upon it; they invest it, mark it, train it, torture it, force it to carry out tasks, to perform ceremonies, to emit signs."[15] Once one understands this, it is not at all strange to consider improvised dance a practice of freedom.[16]

At its core, improvisation demands an ongoing interaction with shifting tight places, whether created by power relations, social norms, aesthetic traditions, or physical technique. Improvised dance literally involves giving shape to oneself and deciding how to move in relation to an unsteady landscape. To go about this endeavor with a sense of confidence and possibility is a powerful way to inhabit one's body and interact with the world. In this sense, improvised dance offers a very real practice of freedom that can be carried into more "pedestrian" spheres of movement, even though, as I have argued throughout the book, there are no guarantees regarding outcome. This is what gives the practice its vitality. Then, in rare instances, as seen in the exquisite moments mentioned in the chapter's opening, improvisers break out well beyond survival. Even if just for a moment—felt in the pressure between throat and ribbon, or the broad expanse of one's chest, or the refusal to strike back or be carried—improvisers alter the terrain of society's tight places, creating thrilling new spaces in which to dance.

Notes

Introduction

1. Margo Nash, "A Teacher Improvising as He Goes," *New York Times,* May 29, 2005.
2. Nash, "Teacher Improvising as He Goes."
3. Lepkoff, "Contact Improvisation/A Definition," 16.
4. Nagrin, *Dance and the Specific Image,* 4.
5. Malone, *Steppin' on the Blues,* 98.
6. "Improvisation in Everyday Life: A Conversation" (panel discussion co-sponsored by Columbia University's World Leaders Forum and the Center for Jazz Studies at Columbia University, Low Memorial Library, Columbia University, New York, September 25, 2007).
7. Orwell, "Politics and the English Language."
8. For further discussion of the difference on this issue between two Truman advisers, Paul Nitze and George Kennan, see N. Thompson, *Hawk and the Dove.*
9. At the 2004 Republican National Convention, President George W. Bush defended the war in Iraq by vaguely extolling the advance of freedom: "The terrorists are fighting freedom with all their cunning and cruelty because freedom is their greatest fear—and they should be afraid, because freedom is on the march." "Text: President Bush's Acceptance Speech to the Republican National Convention," *Washington Post,* September 2, 2004). The president used the terms *free* and *freedom* twenty-two times in his address, anthropomorphizing them while also treating them as transparent and fully formed. Elsewhere in the speech he exclaimed: "Our nation's founding commitment is still our deepest commitment: In our world, and here at home, we will extend the frontiers of freedom." (Ibid.) Although it is hard to discern exactly what *freedom* means in the president's speech, one can characterize his use of the term in several ways: it is a noun, it is concrete and easily identifiable, and it is an unquestioned good that is capable of conquering "evil forces." It also functions as a territory–a place of arrival with expanding borders that are nevertheless clearly defined. This expansionist trope is common (particularly in the United States), and it depends upon the widely held notion

that the land of freedom is a place one not only wishes to expand but also strives to reach. People dream about freedom as if it were an endpoint, the ultimate destination.

10. Porter, *What Is This Thing Called Jazz,* 169.

11. Moten, "Taste Dissonance Flavor Escape," 219.

12. Jacobs, *Incidents in the Life of a Slave Girl,* 348.

13. I am grateful to Fred Moten for mentioning Harriet Jacobs at my dissertation defense at New York University on April 12, 2006. Noting both Jacobs and a moment toward the end of *The History of Sexuality* where Michel Foucault claims, "It is not that life has been totally integrated into techniques that govern and administer it; it constantly escapes them," Moten asked, "What if improvised dance were thought about in relation to escape rather than freedom?" Moten's comments and scholarship have been instrumental in helping me to analyze the ways in which improvisation resists reified notions of freedom. His turn toward escape is a meaningful move that I continue to think about. I look forward to the publication of Moten's upcoming book, *Open Secret.*

14. Foucault, "Ethics of the Concern for Self," 282.

15. Berliner, *Thinking in Jazz,* 1–4.

16. Berliner, *Thinking in Jazz,* 16.

17. Baker, *Turning South Again,* 15.

18. Baker, *Turning South Again,* 69.

19. Baker, *Turning South Again,* 69.

20. Novack, *Sharing the Dance,* 39.

21. Novack, *Sharing the Dance,* 39.

22. Malone, *Steppin' on the Blues,* 34.

23. Malone, *Steppin' on the Blues,* 49.

24. Shay, *Choreophobia,* 11.

25. Shay, *Choreophobia,* 149.

26. Shay, *Choreophobia,* 117–18.

27. Steve Paxton, transcript from Movement 12's Salon Evening with Steve Paxton in Brighton, Feb. 21, 2008, http://www.movement12.org/writings/Steve PaxtonTranscript.pdf.

28. R. Martin, *Critical Moves,* 21.

29. R. Martin, *Critical Moves,* 174.

30. In "Embodying Difference," Jane Desmond argues that moving bodies constitute a primary social text that is complex, meaningful, and always changing. She explains that, whether consciously performed or not, "movement serves as a marker for the production of gender, racial, ethnic, class, and national identities. It can also be read as a signal of sexual identity, age, and illness or health, as well as various other types of distinctions/ descriptions that are applied to individuals or groups." (31) People move their bodies differently across social and cultural groups in different historical moments; it matters whether one occupies a lot of space when one moves or a little, and whether one walks with a swagger or a quiet shuffle.

31. Mauss, "Techniques of the Body," 455.
32. Mauss, "Techniques of the Body," 456.
33. Mauss, "Techniques of the Body," 458.
34. Mauss, "Techniques of the Body," 462.
35. Lepecki, *Exhausting Dance,* 125.
36. Lepecki, "Inscribing Dance," 130.
37. Lepecki, *Exhausting Dance,* 129.
38. Lepecki, "Inscribing Dance," 131.
39. Lepecki, "Inscribing Dance," 135.
40. Lepecki, "Inscribing Dance," 135.
41. Muñoz, *Disidentifications,* 189.
42. Muñoz, *Disidentifications,* 189.
43. Bill Dixon, interview, June 2, 2008.
44. For a thoughtful discussion of these matters, see Muñoz, "Ephemera as Evidence."
45. Banes, *Terpsichore in Sneakers,* xiv.
46. Whereas Banes discusses minimalist sculpture as the modernist art par excellence, Ramsay Burt has recently explained that "the minimalist approach to formalist abstraction was more avant-garde than modernist" (*Judson Dance Theater,* 12). In making this argument, Burt refers to Clement Greenberg and Michael Fried, who famously argued that minimalism's theatricality was antithetical to modernist aesthetic appreciation, where the self-sufficient artwork is available for appreciation in an instantaneous process. See Burt, *Judson Dance Theater,* 12–13.
47. Banes, *Terpsichore in Sneakers,* xv.
48. Manning, *Modern Dance/Negro Dance,* xiii.
49. J. Martin, *Modern Dance,* 1.
50. In a footnote, Manning writes: "In *The Modern Dance* and in his subsequent volumes—America Dancing (New York: Dodge Publishing Company, 1936) and *Introduction to the Dance* (New York: W. W. Norton, 1939; rprt., Brooklyn: Dance Horizons, 1965)—Martin included Isadora Duncan and Ruth St. Denis within the genealogy of modern dance. Nearly all subsequent scholarship (my own included) has followed Martin's usage, even though neither Duncan nor St. Denis ever referred to her practice as modern dance. Nor did Graham, Humphrey, and Tamiris use the term in the late 1920s, when modern dance (a translation of *der moderne Tanz*) connoted the German dance practice associated with Mary Wigman. Only after 1930 did American dancers embrace the term to differentiate their practice from ballet, jazz, and commercial entertainment" (*Modern Dance/Negro Dance,* 223).
51. Several dance scholars have criticized Banes accordingly. See Manning, "Modernist Dogma and Postmodernist Rhetoric"; Burt, *Judson Dance Theater.*
52. J. Martin, *Modern Dance,* 6.
53. See R. Martin, *Critical Moves;* Lepecki, *Exhausting Dance.*
54. R. Martin, *Critical Moves,* 152.
55. See Manning, *Modern Dance/Negro Dance,* xx–xxiv. According to Man-

ning, unlike the story of generational progression within the African American U.S. concert tradition, the historiography of modern and postmodern dance typically progresses via a series of generational rebellions. According to this story, early modern dancers such as Duncan, St. Denis, and Wigman sought alternatives to late-nineteenth-century ballet. Then, after 1930, choreographers such as Martha Graham and Doris Humphrey developed codified movement techniques in an attempt to add formal rigor to the art of dance making. They also grappled with what they considered to be "serious" themes: relations between collectivity and individualism, death, famine, and war. During the 1950s, choreographers such as Merce Cunningham and Alwin Nikolais rejected notions of artistic genius and personal expression and sought random procedures for composition and presentation. Cunningham, greatly influenced by his partner John Cage, was interested in chance procedures (rolling the dice, e.g., or using the *I-ching* to make choreographic decisions) and movement for movement's sake. During the early 1960s, choreographers associated with the legendary Judson Dance Theater, which consisted of a group of artists who studied together and presented free concerts at New York's Judson Memorial Church in the early 1960s, rejected spectacle, traditional hierarchies in dance, and narrow notions of virtuosity, while embracing quotidian movement, nontraditional venues, and improvisation. Manning notes that this reductive narrative appears in books ranging from John Martin's *America Dancing* (1936), to Margaret Lloyd's *The Borzoi Book of Modern Dance* (1949), to Walter Terry's *The Dance in America* (1956), to Don McDonagh's *The Rise and Fall and Rise of Modern Dance* (1970), to Marcia Siegel's *The Shapes of Change* (1979), to Sally Banes's *Terpsichore in Sneakers* (1980, 1987), to Deborah Jowitt's *Time and the Dancing Image* (1988), with hardly any mention of the many African American dancers working at the same time, often in similar ways and in shared spaces.

56. Dils and Albright, *Moving History/Dancing Cultures*, xvi.
57. Dils and Albright, *Moving History/Dancing Cultures*, xvi.
58. Gottschild, *Black Dancing Body*, 8.
59. Gottschild, *Black Dancing Body*, 8.
60. Foster, *Dances That Describe Themselves*, 26–30.
61. Novack, *Sharing the Dance*, 24.
62. Foster, *Dances That Describe Themselves*, 30.
63. Banes, *Greenwich Village 1963*, 3.
64. Banes, *Greenwich Village 1963*, 3.
65. Banes, *Greenwich Village 1963*, 3–4.
66. Banes, *Greenwich Village 1963*, 4.
67. Saul, *Freedom Is, Freedom Ain't*, ix.
68. Saul, *Freedom Is, Freedom Ain't*, ix.
69. Saul, *Freedom Is, Freedom Ain't*, 12.
70. Saul, *Freedom Is, Freedom Ain't*, 12.
71. Saul, *Freedom Is, Freedom Ain't*, 17.
72. Perpener, *African-American Concert Dance*, 205.
73. Bourdieu, *Field of Cultural Production*, 163–64.

74. Bourdieu, *Field of Cultural Production,* 184.
75. Movement Research is a New York dance service organization whose mission is to foster experimentation in dance; in reality it has been and continues to be the face of a specific field. Studies projects are typically panel discussions meant to address issues of dance and social politics. See movementresearch.org for information about the organization and its programming.
76. See Bourdieu, *Distinction;* Bourdieu, *Field of Cultural Production.*
77. Overlie, "Studies Project," 34.
78. R. F. Thompson, "Teaching the People to Triumph over Time," 342.
79. See Moten, *In the Break.*
80. Bill T. Jones, "Hopes and Doubts in the Gestation of a Dance," *New York Times,* Feb. 13, 2000.
81. Foucault, "Ethics of the Concern for Self," 283.
82. Foucault, "Ethics of the Concern for Self," 293.

Chapter 1

1. wa Thiong'o, *Penpoints, Gunpoints, and Dreams,* 41.
2. R. F. Thompson, "Teaching the People to Triumph over Time," 337.
3. R. F. Thompson, "Teaching the People to Triumph over Time," 337.
4. Daniel, "Cuban Dance," 32.
5. Daniel, "Cuban Dance," 31.
6. Daniel, "Cuban Dance," 33. According to Daniel, "These names for dance/music traditions of African descent are mixed geographical, ethnic, religious, and linguistic terms, but the alternate names have survived and are used interchangeably in Cuba." (33)
7. Daniel, "Cuban Dance," 43.
8. Daniel, "Cuban Dance," 44.
9. Daniel, "Cuban Dance," 44.
10. R. F. Thompson, "Teaching the People to Triumph over Time," 337.
11. http://www.state.gov/r/pa/ho/time/id/17341.htm.
12. http://www.state.gov/r/pa/ho/time/id/17341.htm.
13. López, "Of Rhythms and Borders," 317.
14. R. F. Thompson, "Teaching the People to Triumph over Time," 338.
15. Desmond, "Embodying Difference," 41.
16. Dunham, "Thesis Turned Broadway," 215.
17. Dunham, "Thesis Turned Broadway," 214.
18. Manning, "Watching Dunham's Dancing," 260.
19. Clark, "On Stage with the Dunham Company," 285.
20. Aschenbrenner, "Dunham Technique Seminars," 483.
21. Dunham, "Thesis Turned Broadway," 225.
22. R. F. Thompson, "Teaching the People to Triumph over Time," 343–44.
23. R. F. Thompson, "Teaching the People to Triumph over Time," 340.
24. Many thanks to Alex Vázquez for recommending that I read this book.

25. Brock, "Introduction," 10.
26. Brock, "Introduction," 19.
27. Brock, "Introduction," 19.
28. Brock, "Introduction," 22.
29. Delgado and Muñoz, "Rebellions of Everynight Life," 17.
30. Delgado and Muñoz, "Rebellions of Everynight Life," 18.
31. Delgado and Muñoz, "Rebellions of Everynight Life," 18.
32. Dehn, "Papers on Afro-American Social Dance," 35.
33. Eddie Torres, interview by Diane Duggan, New York Public Library's Oral History Project, 19.
34. Torres, interview, 15.
35. Boggs, *Salsiology,* 123.
36. Boggs, *Salsiology,* 98.
37. Boggs, *Salsiology,* 98.
38. Yvonne Daniel notes in "Cuban Dance" that "in the 1930s and 1940s, when Hollywood, the music recording industry, and the general public confused a conga with a tango, a samba with a rumba, North African culture with sub-Saharan culture, Caribbean societies with Latin American societies, they did so out of laziness, ignorance, or bias. There is no excuse today, what with better knowledge of the world, instant technology to correct our errors swiftly, and the will to respect culture distinctiveness." (25). While the term *Latin music and dance* is imprecise, it was the term used at the time, and I will use it in my historical discussion of the Palladium.
39. Salazar, *Mambo Kingdom,* 89.
40. Boggs, *Salsiology,* 128.
41. *Palladium: Where Mambo Was King.*
42. R. F. Thompson, "Teaching the People to Triumph over Time," 340.
43. *Palladium: Where Mambo Was King.*
44. *Palladium: Where Mambo Was King.*
45. *Palladium: Where Mambo Was King.*
46. Salazar, *Mambo Kingdom,* 87.
47. Thomas, *Down These Mean Streets,* 147.
48. Thomas, *Down These Mean Streets,* 105.
49. Thomas, *Down These Mean Streets,* 117.
50. Vega, *When the Spirits Dance Mambo,* 126.
51. Torres, interview, 72.
52. R. F. Thompson, "Teaching the People to Triumph over Time," 341.
53. Dehn, "Papers on Afro-American Social Dance," 34.
54. Dehn, "Papers on Afro-American Social Dance," 34.
55. Boggs, *Salsiology,* 129.
56. Boggs, *Salsiology,* 129.
57. Pedro Aguilar was born in Puerto Rico in 1927, but he was given the name Cuban Pete on a New York dance floor. He usually danced under the name Pete, but one night at the Conga Room, Tommy Morton presented Pete and his dance

partner, Millie Donay, saying, "Here he is again, Pete! No, no, no, CUBAN PETE, King of the Latin Beat," referring to a popular song of the era by Desi Arnaz.

58. *Palladium: Where Mambo Was King.*

59. *Palladium: Where Mambo Was King.*

60. R. F. Thompson, "Teaching the People to Triumph over Time," 341.

61. R. F. Thompson, "Teaching the People to Triumph over Time," 341.

62. Torres, interview, 85.

63. Torres, interview, 21.

64. Dehn, "Papers on Afro-American Social Dance," 33.

65. http://www.dancescape.org/ezine/articles/35/1.

66. http://www.justsalsa.com/culture/mambo/history/articles/alanfeuerstein/mambolegendscubanpeteandmillie/.

67. John S. Wilson, "Ga-Ga Over Cha-Cha," *New York Times,* March 15, 1959.

68. Elden, "Introduction," viii–ix.

69. Lefebvre, *Rhythmanalysis,* 81.

70. Lefebvre, *Rhythmanalysis,* 88.

71. Delgado and Muñoz, "Rebellions of Everynight Life," 13.

72. Delgado and Muñoz, "Rebellions of Everynight Life," 14.

73. Delgado and Muñoz, "Rebellions of Everynight Life," 14.

74. Delgado and Muñoz, "Rebellions of Everynight Life," 14.

75. Vega, *When the Spirits Dance Mambo,* 1.

76. Fischer-Hornung, "Body Possessed," 93.

77. Torres, interview, 66.

78. This discussion emerged as part of an interview conducted by Diane Duggan in three sessions on Aug. 30, Sept. 3, and Oct. 7, 2001. Roberto's last name is not given. The interview is part of the New York Public Library's Oral History Project.

79. Torres, interview, 64.

80. André Lepecki helpfully suggested that I look to Gilles Deleuze when thinking about relations between improvisation and animality. This is a rich area worthy of further exploration. Akira Lippit's *Electric Animal* (2000) and Giorgio Agamben's *The Open* (2002), both of which analyze the defining role of animality in Western philosophy, provide intellectual context for the link between animality and improvisation and illustrate the ethical stakes involved in such an association. Beginning with ancient Greek and Messianic thinkers, and wending his way through modern science and twentieth-century humanism, Agamben notes that man repeatedly has defined his nature in opposition to the animal—a definition that frequently elevates rationality over instinct. Recognizing the force of the "anthropological machine," Agamben argues that we must analyze the constructed division between man and animal anew, recongnizing that the caesura actually exists *within* man. "What," he asks, "is man, if he is always the place—and, at the same time, the result—of ceaseless divisions and caesurae? It is more

urgent to work on these divisions, to ask in what way—within man—has man been separated from non-man, and the animal from the human, than it is to take positions on the great issues, on so-called human rights and values." (16) Here Agamben suggests that analyzing improvisation in relation to animality need not be merely pejorative. Gilles Deleuze suggests something similar with his concept of "becoming-animal." In a discussion of becoming in relation to music, he remarks, "It is not certain whether we can draw a dividing line between animals and human beings: Are there not, as Messiaen believes, musician birds and non-musician birds?" (301) For Deleuze, becoming-animal is not a matter of imitation (where one merely *acts* like a bird or cat), nor is it a matter of representation (where an artist depicts animals in her work). Rather, becoming-animal involves a deterritorialization of the self, a "creative involution" at the level of flows and intensity, where one moves away from majoritarian representations (man, white, old) toward other planes of desire and consistency. See Deleuze and Guattari, *Thousand Plateaus*, in particular the chapter "1730: Becoming-Intense, Becoming-Animal, Becoming-Imperceptible" (232–309). For a discussion of Deleuze in relation to dance, see also Grosz, *Volatile Bodies;* Bogue, *Deleuze on Music, Painting, and the Arts;* Lepecki, *Exhausting Dance.*

81. John Martin, "We Trade Fox Trot for Rumba," *New York Times*, Feb. 6, 1944.

82. J. Martin, "We Trade Fox Trot."

83. Torres, interview, 12.

Chapter 2

1. Robert Farris Thompson mentions this scene briefly in "Teaching the People to Triumph over Time." He claims that a similar "deliberate confusion of roles" occurred during the filming of *Mambo Madness* (1955). Thompson states: "Who knew that in 1955, during the filming of *Mambo Madness* in New York, the entire orchestra of Tito Rodriguez would 'break' and play their mambo in the prone. They took the culturally linked tendencies of Kongo, Lima, and Mexico City as far out as they could" (339).

2. Foster, *Dances That Describe Themselves*, 89.

3. Troupe and Riley, "Remembering Thelonious Monk," 106.

4. Troupe and Riley, "Remembering Thelonious Monk," 106.

5. Bailey, *Improvisation*, 115.

6. Anderson, "Judith Dunn and the Endless Quest," 50.

7. Foster, *Dances That Describe Themselves*, 34.

8. Banes, *Democracy's Body*, 7.

9. Foster, *Dances That Describe Themselves*, 28.

10. Foster, *Dances That Describe Themselves*, 28.

11. Banes, *Democracy's Body*, 19.

12. Banes, *Democracy's Body*, 23.

13. Banes, *Democracy's Body*, 194.

14. Banes, *Democracy's Body,* 198.
15. Banes, *Democracy's Body,* 210.
16. See http://aldotambellini.com/film.html.
17. Dixon, interview, June 2, 2008.
18. Dewar, "'This Is American Music.'"
19. Dewar, "'This Is American Music,'" 18.
20. Young, *Dixonia,* 131.
21. Dixon, interview, June 2, 2008.
22. Young, *Dixonia,* 120.
23. Susan Sgorbati, interview, Bennington, VT, May 31, 2008; Penny Campbell, interview, Shoreham, VT, June 1, 2008.
24. Young, *Dixonia,* 136.
25. Dewar, "'This Is American Music,'" 28.
26. Bill Dixon, interview with Frank Rubolino, Oct. 2002, http://www.one finalnote.com/features/2002/dixon/.
27. Susan Sgorbati, interview, May 31, 2008.
28. See http://emergentimprovisation.org/interview.html, Mar. 29, 2005.
29. Campbell, interview, June 1, 2008.
30. Campbell, interview, June 1, 2008.
31. Anderson, "Judith Dunn and the Endless Quest," 50.
32. Anderson, "Judith Dunn and the Endless Quest," 51.
33. Dunn, "We Don't Talk About It," 12.
34. Young, *Dixonia,* 138–39.
35. Dixon, "To Whom It May Concern," 3.
36. Dixon, interview, June 2, 2008.
37. Dixon, interview, June 2, 2008.
38. Balliett, *Collected Works,* 273.
39. Dixon, interview, June 2, 2008.
40. Dunn, "We Don't Talk About It," 13.
41. Dixon, "Collaboration," 10.
42. Dixon, "Collaboration," 11.
43. Dixon, "Program Statement, Dewhorse," 54.
44. Dixon, "Collaboration," 8.
45. Dixon, "Collaboration," 8.
46. Jowitt, *Time and the Dancing Image,* 312.
47. Anderson, "Judith Dunn and the Endless Quest," 51.
48. Anderson, "Judith Dunn and the Endless Quest," 51.
49. Dixon, "Collaboration," 12.
50. Dixon, "Collaboration," 12.
51. Dixon, "Collaboration," 7.
52. Dixon, "Collaboration," 9.
53. Dixon, "Collaboration," 9.
54. Anderson, "Judith Dunn and the Endless Quest," 51.
55. Dixon, "Program Statement, Dewhorse," 53.

56. J. Martin, *Modern Dance*, 102.

57. J. Martin, *Modern Dance*, 103.

58. Dixon, "Collaboration," 10.

59. Dewar, "'This Is American Music,'" 18.

60. Sgorbati, interview, May 31, 2008; Campbell, interview, June 1, 2008; Dixon, interview, June 2, 2008.

61. Dewar, "'This Is American Music,'" 18.

62. An earlier version of a portion of this article appeared in *Women and Performance: A Journal of Feminist Theory* 17, no. 2 (2007).

63. Muñoz, *Disidentifications*, 1–31.

64. Diane McIntyre, interview with Jennifer Dunning, Apr. 1 and 8, 2000, 32.

65. McIntyre, interview, Apr. 1 and 8, 2000, 32.

66. Muñoz, *Disidentifications*, 15.

67. Muñoz, *Disidentifications*, 17.

68. McIntyre, interview, Apr. 1 and 8, 2000, 33.

69. McIntyre, interview, Apr. 1 and 8, 2000, 34.

70. Quotations from Dianne McIntyre, unless otherwise noted, are from a telephone interview I conducted with her on Mar. 16, 2007.

71. McIntyre, interview, Apr. 1 and 8, 2000, 33.

72. Foster, *Dances That Describe Themselves*, 88.

73. McIntyre, interview, Apr. 1 and 8, 2000, 67.

74. McIntyre, interview, Apr. 1 and 8, 2000, 63.

75. McIntyre, interview, Apr. 1 and 8, 2000, 65.

76. Foster, *Dances That Describe Themselves*, 85.

77. McIntyre, interview, Apr. 1 and 8, 2000, 65.

78. Foster, *Dances That Describe Themselves*, 87.

79. McIntyre, interview, Apr. 1 and 8, 2000, 121–22.

80. McIntyre, interview, Apr. 1 and 8, 2000, 113.

81. Goler, "Dancing Herself," 77.

82. Griffin, *If You Can't Be Free*, 163.

83. Griffin, *If You Can't Be Free*, 163.

84. Griffin, *If You Can't Be Free*, 165.

85. Porter, *What Is This Thing Called Jazz*, 151.

86. Porter, *What Is This Thing Called Jazz*, 153.

87. Porter, *What Is This Thing Called Jazz*, 153.

88. Porter, *What Is This Thing Called Jazz*, 166.

89. Porter, *What Is This Thing Called Jazz*, 167–68.

90. The description of "Triptych" is my own. The Roach quote comes from Porter, *What Is This Thing Called Jazz*, 169.

91. Griffin, *If You Can't Be Free*, 181.

92. Griffin, *If You Can't Be Free*, 181.

93. Griffin, *If You Can't Be Free*, 172.

94. Moten, *In The Break*, 23.

95. Moten, *In the Break*, 22.

96. Griffin, *If You Can't Be Free,* 172.

97. Griffin, *If You Can't Be Free,* 172.

98. *New York Post,* June 13, 1980.

99. Goler, "Dancing Herself," 108.

100. Goler, "Dancing Herself," 108.

101. Foster, *Dances That Describe Themselves,* 30.

102. Goler, "Dancing Herself," 77.

103. Barthes, "The Grain of the Voice," in *Responsibility of Forms,* 276.

104. Barthes, "Grain of the Voice," 277.

105. Barthes, "Grain of the Voice," 276.

106. Barthes, *Pleasure of the Text,* 13.

107. Barthes, "Cy Twombly," in *Responsibility of Forms,* 170.

108. Barthes, "Cy Twombly," 171.

109. Barthes, "Cy Twombly," 171.

110. Barthes, "Cy Twombly," 170.

111. Martin, *The Modern Dance,* 12.

112. Lepecki, *Exhausting Dance,* 6.

113. "Navigating Movements: An Interview with Brian Massumi," by Mary Zournazi, http://www.21cmagazine.com/issue2/massumi.html.

114. Moten, *In the Break,* 207.

115. Moten, *In the Break,* 207.

116. Moten, *In the Break,* 205.

Chapter 3

1. An earlier version of this article appeared in *Dance Research Journal* 39, no. 1 (2007).

2. Branch, *Parting the Waters,* 390.

3. Bruns, *Martin Luther King, Jr,* 55.

4. Branch, *Parting the Waters,* 392.

5. Branch, *Parting the Waters,* 415.

6. Branch, *Parting the Waters,* 415.

7. Branch, *Parting the Waters,* 259.

8. Branch, *Parting the Waters,* 260.

9. Foster, "Choreographies of Protest," 2.

10. Foster, "Choreographies of Protest," 2.

11. Browning, "Choreographing Postcoloniality," 168.

12. Browning, "Choreographing Postcoloniality," 169.

13. Here I am referring to Cynthia Novack's famous book *Sharing the Dance.*

14. Oppenheimer and Lakey, *Manual for Direct Action,* vii.

15. Meier and Rudwick, *Core,* 140.

16. Oppenheimer and Lakey, *Manual for Direct Action,* 93.

17. Oppenheimer and Lakey, *Manual for Direct Action,* 107.

18. Oppenheimer and Lakey, *Manual for Direct Action,* 107.
19. Oppenheimer and Lakey, *Manual for Direct Action,* 112.
20. Oppenheimer and Lakey, *Manual for Direct Action,* 107.
21. Foster, "Choreographies of Protest," 8.
22. Ellison, *Invisible Man,* 456.
23. Ellison, *Invisible Man,* 386.
24. Ellison, *Invisible Man,* 432.
25. King, "Which Way Is Down?" 31.
26. King, "Which Way Is Down?" 35.
27. King, "Which Way Is Down?" 40.
28. King, "Which Way Is Down?" 42.
29. King, "Which Way Is Down?" 42.
30. Volinsky, "Vertical," 257.
31. Volinsky, "Vertical," 255.
32. Volinsky, "Vertical," 256.
33. Volinsky, "Vertical," 257.
34. Kirstein, "Classic Ballet," 239.
35. Stodelle, *Dance Technique of Doris Humphrey,* 20.
36. Stodelle, *Dance Technique of Doris Humphrey,* 14.
37. Stodelle, *Dance Technique of Doris Humphrey,* 15.
38. Gottschild, *Digging the Africanist Presence in American Performance,* 49.
39. Gottschild, *Digging the Africanist Presence in American Performance,* 49.
40. *Evening with the Alvin Ailey American Dance Theater.*
41. Banes, *Democracy's Body,* 121.
42. Novack, *Sharing the Dance,* 61.
43. Paxton, "Small Dance," 23.
44. Paxton, "Fall after Newton," 143.
45. Paxton, "Fall after Newton," 143.
46. Paxton, "Fall after Newton," 142.
47. Novack, *Sharing the Dance,* 79.
48. Stark Smith, "Dealing with the Heat," 91.
49. De Spain, "Moving Decision," 59.
50. Stark Smith, "Dealing with the Heat," 91.
51. Overlie, "Studies Project," 33.
52. Overlie, "Studies Project," 34.
53. Overlie, "Studies Project," 34.
54. Overlie, "Studies Project," 35.
55. Overlie, "Studies Project," 36.
56. Overlie, "Studies Project," 33.
57. Overlie, "Studies Project," 36.
58. Overlie, "Studies Project," 33.
59. Overlie, "Studies Project," 33.
60. Albright, "Open Bodies," 4.
61. Albright, "Open Bodies," 4.

Chapter 4

1. An earlier version of this article appeared in *Dance Research Journal,* vol. 35–36, no. 2–1, Summer (2007).

2. Jennifer Dunning, "Dance: Bodies, Imperfect but Still Moving," *New York Times,* Mar. 10, 2002.

3. Covington, "Is a Beautiful Dance in Itself Enough?"

4. B. T. Jones, "Hopes and Doubts," 1.

5. B. T. Jones and Gillespie, *Last Night on Earth,* 85.

6. B. T. Jones and Gillespie, *Last Night on Earth,* 86.

7. B. T. Jones and Gillespie, *Last Night on Earth,* 116.

8. B. T. Jones and Gillespie, *Last Night on Earth,* 114.

9. B. T. Jones and Gillespie, *Last Night on Earth,* 117.

10. B. T. Jones and Gillespie, *Last Night on Earth,* 117.

11. B. T. Jones and Gillespie, *Last Night on Earth,* 117.

12. B. T. Jones and Gillespie, *Last Night on Earth,* 140.

13. Quotes of Jones talking, along with my description of *Floating the Tongue,* refer to video documentation of *The Breathing Show,* Lincoln Center, July 20, 2000.

14. *The Breathing Show,* Lincoln Center, July 20, 2000.

15. Browning, "Incessant Daily Negotiations," 89.

16. *The Breathing Show,* Lincoln Center, July 20, 2000.

17. B. T. Jones and Gillespie, *Last Night on Earth,* 140.

18. Browning, "Incessant Daily Negotiations," 90.

19. B. T. Jones and Gillespie, *Last Night on Earth,* 141.

20. B. T. Jones and Gillespie, *Last Night on Earth,* 158.

21. Overlie, "Studies Project," 33.

22. B. T. Jones and Gillespie, *Last Night on Earth,* 165.

23. B. T. Jones and Gillespie, *Last Night on Earth,* 164–65.

24. B. T. Jones and Gillespie, *Last Night on Earth,* 165.

25. Jack Anderson, "Dance Festival: 5 Display Experimental Works," *New York Times,* July 13, 1981.

26. B. T. Jones and Gillespie, *Last Night on Earth,* 182.

27. B. T. Jones and Gillespie, *Last Night on Earth,* 197.

28. B. T. Jones and Gillespie, *Last Night on Earth,* 209.

29. Bill T. Jones, interview with Michelle Dent and MJ Thompson, New York University, Mar. 20, 2002.

30. Croce, "Discussing the Undiscussable," 708–19.

31. B. T. Jones, interview, Mar. 20, 2002.

32. B. T. Jones, interview, Mar. 20, 2002.

33. B. T. Jones, interview, Mar. 20, 2002.

34. B. T. Jones, interview, Mar. 20, 2002.

35. Lepecki, "Body in Difference," 13.

36. De Spain, "Digital Dance," 20.

37. Paul Kaiser, http://www.openendedgroup.com/index.php/publications/older-essays/steps/.

38. Paul Kaiser, http://www.openendedgroup.com/index.php/publications/older-essays/steps/.

39. B. T. Jones, interview, Mar. 20, 2002.

40. De Spain, "Dance and Technology," 15.

41. De Spain, "Dance and Technology," 11.

42. Foucault, *History of Sexuality, Volume 2,* 143. Fred Moten brought this moment in Foucault to my attention during my dissertation defense, noting that in some ways "one needed motion capture to figure out what motion capture can't capture."

43. Ross, *No Respect,* 85.

44. Ross, *No Respect,* 85.

45. Barker, *Tremulous Private Body,* viii.

46. De Spain, "Dance and Technology," 6.

47. Feldman, "Human Touch," 224.

48. Marx, *Capital: Volume I,* 532.

49. Marx, *Capital: Volume I,* 526.

50. Feldman, "Human Touch," 248.

51. Feldman, "Human Touch," 244.

52. Feldman, "Human Touch," 246.

53. Feldman, "Human Touch," 246.

54. Feldman, "Human Touch," 249.

55. Marta Braun, *Picturing Time: The Work of Etienne-Jules Marey (1830–1904).* University of Chicago Press, 1995, 14.

56. Braun, *Picturing Time,* 8–41.

57. Braun, *Picturing Time,* 41

58. Braun, *Picturing Time,* 81.

59. De Spain, "Digital Dance," 21.

60. De Spain, "Digital Dance," 21.

61. Croce, "Discussing the Undiscussable," 718.

62. Paul Kaiser, http://www.openendedgroup.com/index.php/publications/older-essays/steps/.

63. The quotes of Jones's talking are from video documentation of *The Breathing Show,* July 20, 2000.

64. B. T. Jones, "Hopes and Doubts," 1.

65. De Spain, "Digital Dance," 20.

66. Baker, *Turning South Again,* 42–43.

67. Baker, *Turning South Again,* 89.

68. B. T. Jones and Gillespie, *Last Night on Earth,* 74.

69. Baker, *Turning South Again,* 43.

70. Gilroy, *Against Race,* 43.

71. Gilroy, *Against Race,* 43.

72. Gilroy, *Against Race,* 47.

73. B. T. Jones, interview, Mar. 20, 2002.
74. Lepecki, "The Body in Difference," 13.

Conclusion

1. Taylor, *Paper Tangos,* xvii.
2. Video documentation of *The Breathing Show,* Lincoln Center, July 20, 2000.
3. Ellison, *Invisible Man,* 59. This quote refers to Jim Trueblood, a character in *Invisible Man,* who states that he had to "move without moving" regarding the incestuous abuse of his daughter. He recounts the incident, explaining: "She's cryin', 'Daddy, Daddy, oh Daddy,' just like that. And all at once I remember the ole lady. She's right beside us snorin' and I can't move 'cause I figgers if I moved it would be a sin. And I figgers too, that if I don't move it maybe ain't no sin, 'cause it happened when I was asleep—although maybe sometimes a man can look at a little ole pigtail gal and see him a whore–you'all know that? Anyway, I realizes that if I don't move the ole lady will see me. I don't want that to happen. That would be *worse* than sin. I'm whisperin' to Matty Lou, tryin' to keep her quiet and I'm figurin' how to git myself out of the fix I'm in without sinnin'. I almost chokes her. 'But once a man gits hisself in a tight spot like that there ain't much he can do. It ain't up to him no longer. There I was, tryin' to git away with all my might, yet having to move *without* movin'. I flew in but I had to walk out. I had to move without movin'." Houston Baker refers to this scene as he develops his discussion of "tight places."
4. Dixon, "Collaboration," 9.
5. Dixon, "Collaboration, 9 (my emphasis).
6. Nehamas, *Art of Living,* 174.
7. Nehamas, *Art of Living,* 175.
8. Foucault, "Ethics of the Concern for Self," 292.
9. Foucault, "Ethics of the Concern for Self," 287.
10. Foucault, "Technologies of the Self," 239.
11. See Foucault, "Technologies of the Self," 238–42.
12. Foucault, "On the Genealogy of Ethics," 261. This writing was the product of interviews and conversations that Paul Rabinow and Hubert Dreyfus conducted with Michel Foucault in Apr. 1983.
13. Nehamas, *Art of Living,* 178.
14. Foucault,"What Is Enlightenment?" 316.
15. Foucault, "Body of the Condemned," 172–73.
16. For some, the question remains as to whether these practices—understood as technologies of the self—relate to politics in a meaningful way. To what extent can focus on the self, no matter how artful or full of care, affect a social world? Is it not a selfish endeavor at odds with collectivity? No. According to Foucault, the ancient notion of care involved a deep exploration of the constraints of one's time and was not at all antithetical to the notion of social world or vibrant civil

society. Nehamas grasps this relationship and argues that in Foucault's late work, "the private and the public, the aesthetic and the political, are as entangled with one another as the 'life' and the 'work.'" He goes on to argue, "By turning to the self in his later works and by living in a way consonant with his ideas, Foucault finally managed to express his 'deep love' for the excluded and the marginalized in practical terms." See Nehamas, *Art of Living,* 177–87.

Of course, practices of freedom must be both multiple and temporary because the world is always shifting and the self is never finished. Likewise, any notion of collectivity associated with improvisation must be temporary. As Foucault explains when discussing problematization:

> I do not appeal to any "we"—to any of those "*wes*" whose consensus, whose values, whose traditions constitute the framework for a thought and define the conditions in which it can be validated. . . . Because it seems to me that the "we" must not be previous to the question; it can only be the result—and the necessarily temporary result—of the question as it is posed in the new terms in which one formulates it.

See Foucault, "Polemics, Politics, and Problematizations," 114.

Bibliography

Agamben, Giorgio. *The Open: Man and Animal.* Trans. Kevin Attell. Stanford: Stanford University Press, 2004.

Albright, Ann Cooper. "Open Bodies: (X)Changes of Identity in Capoeira and Contact Improvisation." In *CORD 2001: Transmigratory Moves: Dance in Global Circulation,* 1–7, ed. Janice LaPointe-Crump. New York: New York University Press, 2001.

Anderson, Jack. "Judith Dunn and the Endless Quest." *Dance Magazine,* November 1967: 48–51, 66–67.

Aschenbrenner, Joyce. "Dunham Technique Seminars." In Clark and Johnson, *Kaiso!,* 481–87.

Bailey, Derek. *Improvisation: Its Nature and Practice in Music.* New York: Da Capo Press, 1992.

Baker, Houston. *Turning South Again: Re-Thinking Modernism/Re-Reading Booker T.* Durham: Duke University Press, 2001.

Balliett, Whitney. *Collected Works: A Journal of Jazz 1954–2001.* New York: St. Martin's Press, 2000.

Banes, Sally. *Democracy's Body: Judson Dance Theater, 1962–1964.* Durham: Duke University Press, 1993.

Banes, Sally. *Greenwich Village 1963: Avant-Garde Performance and the Effervescent Body.* Durham: Duke University Press, 1993.

Banes, Sally. *Terpsichore in Sneakers: Post-Modern Dance.* Wesleyan: Wesleyan University Press, 1987.

Barker, Francis. *The Tremulous Private Body: Essays on Subjection.* Ann Arbor: University of Michigan Press, 1995.

Barthes, Roland. *The Pleasure of the Text.* Trans. Richard Miller. New York: Hill and Wang, 1975.

Barthes, Roland. *The Responsibility of Forms.* Trans. Richard Howard. Berkeley: University of California Press, 1985.

Benjamin, Walter. "The Work of Art in the Age of Mechanical Reproduction." In *Illuminations,* 217–52. New York: Harcourt Brace Jovanovich, Inc., 1968.

Berliner, Paul. *Thinking in Jazz: The Infinite Art of Improvisation.* Chicago: University of Chicago Press, 1994.

Boggs, Vernon. *Salsiology: Afro-Cuban Music and the Evolution of Salsa in New York City.* Westport: Greenwood Press, 1992.

Bogue, Ronald. *Deleuze on Music, Painting, and the Arts.* New York: Routledge, 2003.

Bourdieu, Pierre. *Distinction.* Cambridge, MA: Harvard University Press, 1984.

Bourdieu, Pierre. *The Field of Cultural Production: Essays on Art and Literature.* Ed. and intro. Randal Johnson. New York: Columbia University Press, 1993.

Branch, Taylor. *Parting the Waters: America in the King Years, 1954–63.* New York: Touchstone, 1988.

Brock, Lisa. "Introduction: Between Race and Empire." In *Between Race and Empire: African-Americans and Cubans before the Cuban Revolution,* 1–32, ed. Lisa Brock and Digna Castañeda Fuertes. Philadelphia: Temple University Press, 1998.

Browning, Barbara. "Choreographing Postcoloniality: Reflections on the Passing of Edward Said." *Dance Research Journal* (Winter 2003, Summer 2004).

Browning, Barbara. "Incessant Daily Negotiations: Bill T. Jones's *Floating the Tongue.*" *Drama Review* 49, no. 2 (2005): 164–69.

Bruns, Roger. *Martin Luther King, Jr: A Biography.* Westport: Greenwood Press, 2006.

Burt, Ramsay. *Judson Dance Theater: Performative Traces.* London and New York: Routledge, 2006.

Clark, VèVè. "On Stage with the Dunham Company: An Interview with Vanoye Aikens." In Clark and Johnson, *Kaiso!,* 274–87.

Clark, VèVè, and Sara E. Johnson, eds. *Kaiso! Writings by and about Katherine Dunham.* Madison: University of Wisconsin Press, 2006.

Copeland, Roger, and Marshall Cohen, eds. *What Is Dance: Readings in Theory and Criticism.* Oxford: Oxford University Press, 1983.

Covington, Richard. "Is a Beautiful Dance in Itself Enough?" *Salon,* March 28, 1997. http://www.salon.com/march97/jones970328.html

Croce, Arlene. "Discussing the Undiscussable." In *Writing in the Dark, Dancing in the New Yorker,* 708–19. New York: Farrar, Straus, and Giroux, 2000.

Daly, Ann. "Bill T. Jones in Conversation with Ann Daly." In *Art Performs Life: Merce Cunningham/Meredith Monk/Bill T. Jones,* 118–24, exhibition catalogue. Minneapolis: Walker Art Center, 1998.

Daniel, Yvonne. "Cuban Dance: An Orchard of Caribbean Creativity." In Sloat, *Caribbean Dance from Abakua to Zouk,* 23–55.

Davis, Angela. *Blues Legacies and Black Feminism: Gertrude "Ma" Rainey, Bessie Smith, and Billie Holiday.* New York: Pantheon Books, 1998.

Dehn, Mura. "Papers on Afro-American Social Dance, ca. 1869–1987." Performing Arts Research Collection—Dance. New York: New York Public Library for the Performing Arts.

Deleuze, Gilles, and Felix Guattari. *A Thousand Plateaus: Capitalism and Schizophrenia*. Trans. Brian Massumi. Minneapolis: University of Minnesota Press, 1987.

Delgado, Celeste Fraser, and José Esteban Muñoz, eds. *Everynight Life: Culture and Dance in Latin/O America*. Durham: Duke University Press, 1997.

Delgado, Celeste Fraser, and José Esteban Muñoz. "Rebellions of Everynight Life." In Delgado and Muñoz, *Everynight Life*, 9–32.

De Man, Paul. "Aesthetic Formalization: Kleist's Ubber die Marionnettentheater." In *The Rhetoric of Romanticism*, 263–90. New York: Columbia University Press, 1984.

Desmond, Jane. "Embodying Difference: Issues in Dance and Cultural Studies." In *Meaning In Motion: New Cultural Studies of Dance*, ed. Jane C. Desmond. Durham: Duke University Press, 1997.

De Spain, Kent. "Dance and Technology: A Pas de Deux for Post-Humans." *Dance Research Journal* 32, no. 1 (2000): 2–17.

De Spain, Kent. "Digital Dance: The Computer Artistry of Paul Kaiser." *Dance Research Journal* 32, no. 1 (2000): 18–23.

De Spain, Kent. "A Moving Decision: Notes on the Improvising Mind." *Contact Quarterly* 20, no. 1 (1995): 48–50.

Dewar, Andrew Raffo. "'This Is American Music': Aesthetics, Music and Visual Art of Bill Dixon." Master's thesis, Wesleyan University, 2004.

Dils, Ann, and Ann Cooper Albright, eds. *Moving History/Dancing Cultures: A Dance History Reader*. Middletown: Wesleyan University Press, 2001.

Dixon, Bill. "Collaboration: 1965–1972: Judith Dunn—Dancer/Choreographer, Bill Dixon—Musician/Composer." *Contact Quarterly* 10, no. 2 (1985): 7–12.

Dixon, Bill. "Program Statement, Dewhorse." In *L'Opera: A Collection of Letters, Writings, Musical Scores, Drawings, and Photographs (1967–1986) [Volume One]*. North Bennington, Metamorphosis Music, BMI, 53–55.

Dixon, Bill. "To Whom It May Concern." *Coda* 8, no. 4 (1967): 2–10.

Dunham, Katherine. "Thesis Turned Broadway." In Clark and Johnson, *Kaiso!*, 214–16.

Dunn, Judith. "We Don't Talk About It, We Engage It." *Eddy*, no. 2 (January 1974): 10–14.

Elden, Stuard. "Introduction." In *Rhythmanalysis: Space, Time, and Everyday Life*, by Henri Lefebvre, vii–xv. London: Continuum, 2004.

Ellison, Ralph. *Invisible Man*. New York: Vintage International, 1947.

An Evening with the Alvin Ailey American Dance Theater. 1986. DVD. Dir. Thomas Grimm. Image Entertainment, January 23, 2001.

Feldman, Allen. "The Human Touch: Towards a Historical Anthropology and Dream Analysis of Self-Acting Instruments." In *ReMembering the Body*, ed. Gabriele Brandstetter and Hortensia Volckers, 224–59. Ostfildern, Germany: Hatje Cantz Verlag, 2000.

Fischer-Hornung, Dorothea. "The Body Possessed: Katherine Dunham Dance

Technique in Mambo." In *Embodying Liberation: The Black Body in American Dance,* ed. Dorothea Fischer-Hornung and Alison D. Goeller, 91–112. Hamburg: Transaction Publishers, 2001.

Foster, Susan. "Choreographies of Protest." *Theatre Journal* 55, no. 3 (2003): 395–412.

Foster, Susan. *Dances That Describe Themselves: The Improvised Choreography of Richard Bull.* Middletown: Wesleyan University Press, 2002.

Foster, Susan. "Taken by Surprise: Improvisation in Dance and Mind." In *Taken by Surprise: A Dance Improvisation Reader,* ed. Ann Cooper Albright and David Gere, 3–10. Middletown: Wesleyan University Press.

Foucault, Michel. "The Body of the Condemned." In *Foucault Reader,* 170–78.

Foucault, Michel. *Discipline and Punish: The Birth of the Prison.* Trans. Alan Sheridan. New York: Vintage Books, 1977.

Foucault, Michel. "The Ethics of the Concern for Self as a Practice of Freedom." In Rabinow, *Ethics,* 281–301.

Foucault, Michel. *The Foucault Reader.* Ed. Paul Rabinow. New York: Pantheon Books, 1984.

Foucault, Michel. *The History of Sexuality, Volume 2.*

Foucault, Michel. "On the Genealogy of Ethics: An Overview of Work in Progress." In Rabinow, *Ethics,* 253–80.

Foucault, Michel. "Polemics, Politics, and Problematizations." In Rabinow, *Ethics,* 111–19.

Foucault, Michel. *Power/Knowledge: Selected Interviews and Other Writings, 1972–1977.* Ed. Colin Gordon. New York: Pantheon Books, 1972.

Foucault, Michel. "Technologies of the Self." In Rabinow, *Ethics,* 223–51.

Foucault, Michel. "What Is Enlightenment?" In Rabinow, *Ethics,* 303–19.

Franko, Mark. *Dancing Modernism/Performing Politics.* Bloomington: Indiana University Press, 1995.

Gilroy, Paul. *Against Race: Imagining Political Culture beyond the Color Line.* Cambridge: Belknap Press of Harvard University Press, 2000.

Goler, Veta. "Dancing Herself: Choreography, Autobiography, and the Expression of the Black Woman Self in the Work of Dianne McIntyre, Blondell Cummings, and Jawole Willa Jo Zollar." Master's thesis, Emory University, 1994.

Gottschild, Brenda Dixon. *The Black Dancing Body: A Geography from Coon to Cool.* New York: Palgrave Macmillan, 2005.

Gottschild, Brenda Dixon. *Digging the Africanist Presence in American Performance.* Westport: Greenwood Press, 1996.

Griffin, Farah Jasmine. *If You Can't Be Free, Be a Mystery: In Search of Billie Holiday.* New York: Free Press, 2001.

Grosz, Elizabeth. *Volatile Bodies: Toward a Corporeal Feminism.* Bloomington and Indianapolis: Indiana University Press, 1994.

Jacobs, Harriet. *Incidents in the Life of a Slave Girl.* New York: Modern Library, 2000.

Jones, Bill T., and Peggy Gillespie. *Last Night on Earth*. New York: Pantheon Books, 1995.

Jones, Gayle. *Corregidora*. Boston: Beacon Press, 1975.

Joseph, Miranda. *Against the Romance of Community*. Minneapolis: University of Minnesota Press, 2002.

Jowitt, Deborah. *Time and the Dancing Image*. New York: William Morrow and Co., 1988.

King, Jason. "Which Way Is Down? Improvisations on Black Mobility." *Women and Performance: A Journal of Feminist Theory*, 14:1, no. 27 (2004): 25–45.

Kirstein, Lincoln. "Classic Ballet: Aria of the Aerial." In Copeland and Cohen, *What Is Dance*, 238–43.

Lefebvre, Henri. *Rhythmanalysis: Space, Time, and Everyday Life*. Trans. Stuart Elden and Gerald Moore. London: Continuum, 2004.

Lepecki, André. "The Body in Difference." *FAMA* 1, no. 1 (2000): 6–13.

Lepecki, André. *Exhausting Dance: Performance and the Politics of Movement*. New York and London: Routledge Taylor and Francis Group, 2006.

Lepecki, André. "Inscribing Dance." In *Of the Presence of the Body: Essays on Dance and Performance Theory*, ed. André Lepecki. Middletown: Wesleyan University Press, 2004.

Lepkoff, Daniel. "Contact Improvisation/A Definition." In Nelson and Stark Smith, *Sourcebook*, 16.

Lippit, Akira. *Electric Animal: Toward a Rhetoric of Wildlife*. Minneapolis: University of Minnesota Press, 2000.

López, Ana. "Of Rhythms and Borders." In Delgado and Muñoz, *Everynight Life*, 310–44.

Mackey, Nathaniel. *Paracritical Hinge: Essays, Talks, Notes, Interviews*. Madison: University of Wisconsin Press, 2005.

Malone, Jacqui. *Steppin' on the Blues: The Visible Rhythms of African American Dance*. Champaign: University of Illinois Press, 1996.

Manning, Susan. *Modern Dance/Negro Dance: Race in Motion*. Minneapolis: University of Minnesota Press, 2004.

Manning, Susan. "Modernist Dogma and Postmodernist Rhetoric." *TDR: The Drama Review* 32 (4) (1998): 32–39.

Manning, Susan. "Watching Dunham's Dances, 1937–1945." In Clark and Johnson, *Kaiso!*, 256–66.

Martin, John. *The Modern Dance*. New York: A. S. Barnes & Co., Inc., 1933.

Martin, Randy. *Critical Moves: Dance Studies in Theory and Politics*. Durham: Duke University Press, 1998.

Mauss, Marcel. "Techniques of the Body." In *Incorporations*, ed. Jonathan Crary and Sanford Kwinter, 454–77. New York: Zone, 1992.

Marx, Karl. *Capital: Volume I*. London: Penguin Books, 1976.

Meier, August, and Elliott Rudwick. *Core: A Study in the Civil Rights Movement, 1942–1968*. Oxford: Oxford University Press, 1973.

Monson, Ingrid, Daniel Fischlin, and Ajay Heble, eds. *The Other Side of*

Nowhere: Jazz, Improvisation, and Communities in Dialogue. Middletown: Wesleyan University Press, 2004.

Moore, Robin. *Nationalizing Blackness: Afrocubanismo and Artistic Revolution in Havana, 1920–1940.* Pittsburgh: University of Pittsburgh Press, 1997.

Moten, Fred. *In the Break: The Aesthetics of the Black Radical Tradition.* Minneapolis: University of Minnesota Press, 2003.

Moten, Fred. "Taste Dissonance Flavor Escape: Preface for a Solo by Miles Davis." *Women and Performance: A Journal of Feminist Theory* 17, no. 2 (2007): 217–46.

Muñoz, José. *Disidentifications: Queers of Color and the Performance of Politics.* Minneapolis: University of Minnesota Press, 1999.

Muñoz, José. "Ephemera as Evidence: Introductory Notes to Queer Acts." *Women and Performance: A Journal of Feminist Theory* 8:2, no. 16 (1996): 5–16.

Nagrin, Daniel. *Dance and the Specific Image: Improvisation.* Pittsburgh: Pittsburgh University Press, 1994.

Nehamas, Alexander. *The Art of Living: Socratic Reflections from Plato to Foucault.* Berkeley: University of California Press, 2000.

Nelson, Lisa, and Nancy Stark Smith, eds. *Sourcebook: Collected Writings and Graphics from* Contact Quarterly Dance Journal *1975–1992.* Northampton: Contact Editions, 1997.

Novack, Cynthia. *Sharing the Dance: Contact Improvisation and American Culture.* Madison: University of Wisconsin Press, 1990.

Oppenheimer, Martin, and George Lakey. *A Manual for Direct Action.* Foreword by Bayard Rustin. Chicago: Quadrangle Books, 1964.

Orwell, George. "Politics and the English Language." http://www.orwell.ru/library/essays/politics/english/e_polit.

Overlie, Mary. "The Studies Project." *Contact Quarterly* 9, no. 3 (1984): 30–37.

The Palladium: Where Mambo Was King. Kaufman Films, 2003. Directed by Kevin Kaufman.

Paxton, Steve. "Fall after Newton." In Nelson and Stark Smith, *Sourcebook,* 42–43.

Paxton, Steve. "The Small Dance." Elizabeth Zimmer interviewing Steve Paxton. In Nelson and Stark Smith, *Sourcebook,* 23.

Perpener, John. *African-American Concert Dance.* Chicago: University of Illinois Press, 2001.

Phelan, Peggy. *Unmarked: The Politics of Performance.* New York: Routledge, 1993.

Porter, Eric. *What Is This Thing Called Jazz: African American Musicians as Artists, Critics, and Activists.* Berkeley: University of California Press, 2002.

Rabinow, Paul, ed. *Ethics: Subjectivity and Truth.* New York: New Press, 1997

Ross, Andrew. *No Respect: Intellectuals and Popular Culture.* New York: Routledge, 1989.

Salazar, Max. *Mambo Kingdom: Latin Music in New York, 1926–1990.* New York: Schirmer Books, 2002.

Saul, Scott. *Freedom Is, Freedom Ain't: Jazz and the Making of the Sixties.* Cambridge: Harvard University Press, 2003.

Shay, Anthony. *Choreophobia: Solo Improvised Dance in the Iranian World.* Costa Mesa: Mazda Publishers, 1999.

Sloat, Susanna, ed. *Caribbean Dance from Abakua to Zouk: How Movement Shapes Identity.* Tampa: University Press of Florida, 2002.

Stark Smith, Nancy. "Dealing with the Heat." *Contact Quarterly* 9, no. 3 (1984): 3.

Stodelle, Ernestine. *The Dance Technique of Doris Humphrey and Its Creative Potential.* 2nd ed. Princeton: Princeton Book Company, 1978.

Taylor, Julie. *Paper Tangos.* Durham: Duke University Press, 1998.

Thomas, Piri. *Down These Mean Streets.* New York: Vintage, 1997.

Thompson, Nicholas. *The Hawk and the Dove.* New York: Henry Holt & Company, Incorporated, 2009.

Thompson, Robert Farris. "Teaching the People to Triumph over Time." In Sloat, *Caribbean Dance from Abakua to Zouk,* 336–44.

Troupe, Quincy, and Ben Riley. "Remembering Thelonious Monk: When the Music Was Happening Then He'd Get Up and Do His Little Dance." In *The Jazz Cadence of American Culture,* 102–13. ed. Robert G. O'Meally. New York: Columbia University Press, 1998.

Vega, Marta. *When the Spirits Dance Mambo: Growing Up Nyuorican in El Barrio.* New York: Three Rivers Press, 2004.

Volinsky, A. K. "The Vertical: The Fundamental Principle of Classic Dance." In Copeland and Cohen, *What Is Dance,* 255–57.

wa Thiong'o, Ngugi. *Penpoints, Gunpoints, and Dreams: Towards a Critical Theory of the Arts.* Oxford: Clarendon Press, 1996.

Young, Ben, comp. *Dixonia: A Bio-Discography of Bill Dixon.* Westport: Greenwood Press, 1998.

Index